A WORKBOOK FOR THE MIDDLE YEARS

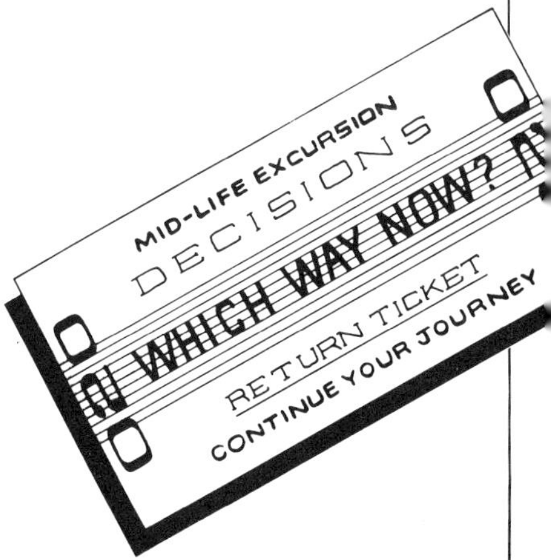

Publishers

Lifeskills
PUBLISHING
GROUP

Clarendon Chambers, 51 Clarendon Road, Leeds LS2 9NZ.
Tel: 0532 467128

British Library Cataloguing in Publications Data
Smith, Maggie
The Best is Yet to Come: (a workbook for the middle years)
1. Great Britain. Careers. Change. Manuals
1. Title
331. 7'20'0941

ISBN 0–90 70 42–30–9

Originally published as "Branching Out".

Revised and rewritten by Maggie Smith and Penny Mares Associates.

Design and Layout by Thompson Designs.
Typeset by Hunters Armley Ltd., Leeds.
Printed by Walker & Carson.

CONTENTS

CHAPTER 1

INTRODUCTION

HOW CAN THIS WORKBOOK HELP ME?

AN ANALYSIS OF THE AREAS OF CONCERN IN MY LIFE NOW.

This chapter offers an introduction to the workbook and analyses common factors which may influence your life as you reach the middle years. It suggests questions you may need to address. There is an exercise which will help you to see where the book can help you and will pinpoint specific areas of uncertainty. The structure of the book is explained in detail, together with an explanation of the value of planning this next stage of your life.

Who will benefit from using this book?

- People whose job has been 'reorganised'
- People who are considering leaving work – through voluntary severance; redundancy; early retirement, etc.
- Women returning to work after child rearing
- People who would like to run their own businesses
- Anyone who thinks life could offer more!

How do you make the decision?

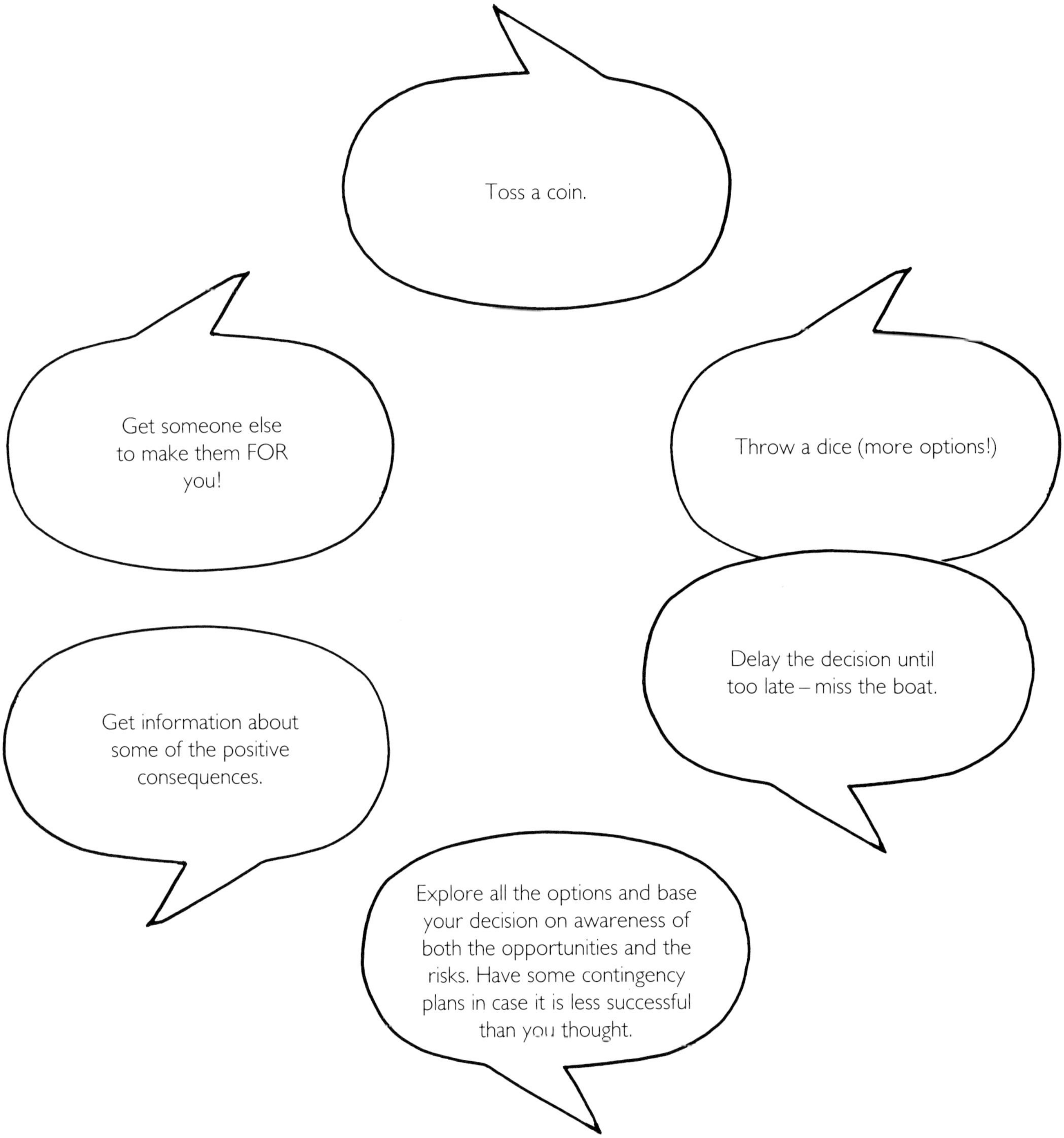

The last way is most likely to lead to satisfaction!

EXERCISE 1

FACING THE DECISION

Exercise 1 will show how well equipped you are to make an informed choice.

What To Do: Circle the letters beside the answers that you identify with most.

1 How much choice do I have in the decision I need to make?	A Total – I initiated a request for the change B Almost total – I feel free to decide C Under some pressure D Hobson's choice really E None – compulsory
2 How much time is there?	A Five years B Six months C Six weeks D Two days E Have not been thinking about it
3 How financially viable must it be?	A A better-paid job planned B No change C Need to earn small sum D Need to earn same as before E Haven't worked it out yet
4 How will it affect other people in my life?	A I talk things over with everyone to see how they feel B My partner and my family share in my decisions C Haven't discussed it much D We don't agree about the future E There are very few to ask
5 Am I sure I know how to cope with major change?	A I know this is a major decision which might be unexpectedly upsetting B I'm surprised how scared I feel, even though I'm looking forward to it C It's something I'll have to learn to accept D Only pessimists see problems E New situations never affect me
6 How do I plan to spend my time?	A Have made plans, but left space to revise them regularly B Would welcome suggestions C Looking for another job D So many ideas, I don't know where to fit them in E No idea
7 I face my middle years with.....	A Confidence – I've examined all the possibilities B Pleasure and slight apprehension C Great excitement D Some anxiety E Dread

What To Do Next: Add up your score: A = 5
B = 4
C = 3
D = 2
E = 1

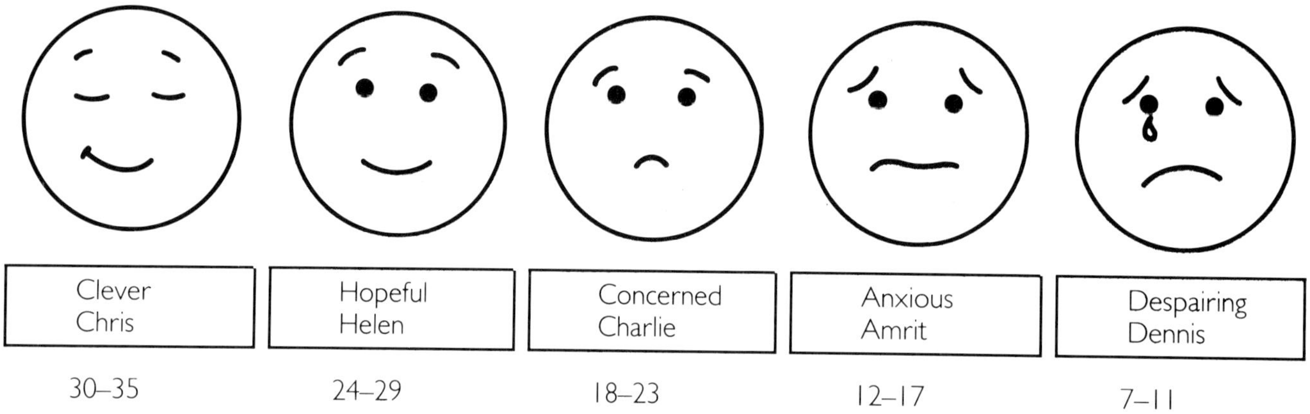

Which face of decision is yours?

If you are a Clever Chris, you will be glad to have even more resources to help you complete your plans. Most people score between 19 and 25 the first time they complete this exercise.

You may have been surprised by the low score for:

5D No problems
6D So many ideas
7C Great excitement

This is because you may not have thought beyond the immediate prospect and are denying the reality of the change. You can read more about this in Chapter 3 – The Management of Change. When you have completed as much of the book as you want to, please return to this exercise to see how your score has changed.

How do I use this book? What can I expect to gain? Why do I need to make plans?

In each chapter you will find *Exercises.*
Facts.
Information.
Resources.

Exercises

The exercises are the core element of the book – they will help you to work out for yourself how you will manage transition by enabling you:

- to analyse how your life experiences have influenced the way you react to change.
- to clarify who will be part of your future and where you will live.
- to discover any differences between what you *want* and what you really *need.*
- to discover your skills, values and interests.
- to decide whether or not self-employment would satisfy you.
- to check how healthy your lifestyle is.
- to manage any setbacks.

Information and facts

The factual information will give you material to aid your decision making, and will explain some of the background including:

- why the middle years are an important transition
- how patterns of work are changing
- how womens' experiences differ from mens'
- how to look for another job
- how life-changes affect people
- connections between change – stress – ill-health
- ways to manage stress and maintain good health
- suggestions for leisure – learning – unpaid work – retraining

Resources

The final chapter contains a book list and the addresses of organisations which offer detailed information about areas of particular interest to you.

How do I use the book?

Although each chapter is designed to lead into the next, with a progress summary at the end of each chapter which assumes you are building your picture from the beginning, it is not essential to work through the exercises in sequence.

Some decisions will obviously be dependent upon others. It is quite possible that you will use the book only to look for general information – job hunting, voluntary work, travel facilities. The disadvantage of this approach is that you may be surprised and distressed by your inability to enjoy your time fully.

You may at this stage choose to look for information plus advice – Where can I make myself useful? How can I plan my time? Where do I get trained? Where do I find another job?

You are beginning to understand that you need to plan, but may still be unaware of all factors involved in the change, and all the opportunities to complete some of the exercises at this stage.

Working systematically through the book, exploring your approach to your life so far and using it to understand the present, will take longer, but will in the end save you time.

For example, if you plan to become self-employed, you may look first at page 116 Becoming self-employed.

You will then need to think about: time management
who else is involved
small businesses
financial assistance

However, if you have first analysed your values and your skills, you will have discovered if you are likely to enjoy being self-employed. It is not a way of life for those who value security!

Each exercise is clearly presented and will refer you to other relevant sections.

As you complete the exercises and compare them, you will be building up a picture of yourself when you are most effective and in charge of your life.

It is important to discuss your findings with other people – they often see points you may have missed, and may encourage you to be more positive about your skills, etc!

If possible, work through the book with the person, or people, most likely to be affected by any choices you make, you may gain a new perspective on your relationships.

Talk to as many people as possible, especially those who have had similar experiences – it will add to your information.

Make notes as you go along – there will be suggestions about the most effective way to use your information, but it is YOUR book, YOUR transition, YOUR future. Do not hesitate to adapt it to your own circumstances.

How can reviewing the past help me to plan the future?

We learn from our experiences, so reviewing the past may prevent repetition of an error and highlight vulnerable spots. There is evidence that people who prepare for change adjust quicker.

There are patterns in our behaviour and our response to events which are developed through life experiences. Analysing some of those experiences helps to make sense of the present and facilitates more informed choices. You probably have 30–40 years of active life ahead – time for a new career, a new life. To make a success of those years and to live as fully as possible, find out what you want and what you enjoy.

Your interests, wishes and happiness determine what you actually do well, more than your intelligence, aptitude and skills do.

R N Bolles

This may be the opportunity you have been seeking to design your own future . . . . .

A ROUND TUIT
AT LAST WE HAVE
A SUFFICIENT QUANITITY FOR
EACH OF YOU TO HAVE ONE. GUARD
IT WITH YOUR LIFE! THESE TUITS HAVE
BEEN VERY HARD TO COME BY, ESPECIALLY
THE ROUND ONES. THIS IS AN INDISPENSABLE
ITEM. IT WILL ENABLE YOU TO BECOME MORE
EFFICIENT. FOR YEARS WE HAVE HEARD PEOPLE
SAYING; *I'LL DO IT AS SOON AS I GET A ROUND*
TUIT! NOW THAT YOU HAVE A ROUND TUIT OF
YOUR OWN MANY THINGS THAT HAVE
NEEDED TO BE ACCOMPLISHED
WILL NOW GET DONE.

Many of us are not consciously aware of planning our lives. How much planning went into your choice of: your last job; your home; your car; your last holiday?

Even people who like to go on unplanned holidays usually know how to get to their destination, what the weather is likely to be like and probably how long they will be away.

Using the same metaphor, this book is not a total package tour with every visit timetabled – it provides maps and guidebooks and glimpses of possible hazards on the journey!

You can begin this journey by seeing if you can afford it!

GOOD LUCK!

The most that we can hope to do is to train every individual to realise all his/her potentialities and become completely him/herself

Aldous Huxley

CHAPTER 2

HOW DO I FEEL ABOUT MY FUTURE? CAN I AFFORD TO CHANGE?

HOW MUCH MONEY WILL I HAVE?

HOW MUCH WILL I NEED?

WHERE WILL IT COME FROM?

The first question most people ask facing a major life-change is "What will it cost?" It may be useful to analyse your general financial position before considering the other issues.

This chapter will help you to clarify what you really want, rather than what you think you need – not just financially, but in the other areas of your life; to explore how you feel about the transition you face; and to analyse what factors in your job you want to keep, (or to lose).

> *"Annual income twenty pounds, annual expenditure nineteen nineteen six, result happiness. Annual income twenty pounds, annual expenditure twenty pounds ought and six, result misery"*

Charles Dickens; David Copperfield

It is natural to wonder if a radical change in lifestyle will cause financial pressures, and important to decide how much you want to earn. You need to analyse:

how much you will have;
how much you will need;
where it will come from.

Questions to ask about 'leaving money'.

If you are planning to leave your present job, obtain a detailed breakdown of any money to which you may be entitled. This is especially important if your decision involves voluntary severence, redundancy, early retirement, etc. If you need to leave through ill-health you MAY be entitled to your full occupational pension, but the D.S.S. interpretation of 'medical grounds' may differ from your employer's, and regulations about severance terms and employee pension schemes differ in every organisation. The details are often complex and it is advisable to talk to someone, probably in personnel, with expertise in this field.

DO REMEMBER THAT LEGISLATION CAN CHANGE RAPIDLY: CHECK THAT YOUR INFORMATION ON STATUTORY ENTITLEMENTS AND REQUIREMENTS IS UP-TO-DATE.

Questions to ask yourself about savings:

- How much cash should I reserve for emergencies?
- Do I want income from savings to supplement my other income?
- How many years do I intend to continue earning?
- What is my future tax position likely to be?

You have managed your finances for many years, and we are not suggesting that you need to learn to budget, but it could be fun to forecast and perhaps make some pleasant discoveries!

The budget checklists on the next page probably contain items which will not be relevant to you, and spaces have been left for any items which have been omitted. It is not intended as a compulsory, binding budget, merely an aid to a general overview of your finances and a pointer to adjustments you may need to make.

Remember:

Needs may change.
Circumstances may change.
Legislation may change.
Crises may occur.

Could we manage without two cars/two homes/ two incomes? How will we face the neighbours?

We pay everything by monthly banker's order – plan essentials, do what we like with the rest.

Different attitudes to money!

Budgeting. . . . .present, future, post retirement

You may find it helpful to make several estimates. After retiring, review the checklist after six months or so, as circumstances change. Look carefully at your present expenditure.

For example, if you have private health care, who pays for it, and how often have you needed to use it?
How much is essential – how much a 'luxury' item?

I INCOME	PRESENT	IF I CHANGE MY ROLE
Regular pay		
Bonuses		
Overtime		
Commission		
Interest on savings		
Company car/van		
Company/tied housing		
Pension		
Child benefit		
Unemployment benefit		
Single parent allowance		
Supplementary benefit		
Disability pension		
Widow's pension		
Other		
	TOTAL..................	TOTAL..................

2 EXPENDITURE	PRESENT	IF I CHANGE MY ROLE
N I contribution		
Pension scheme		
Income tax		
Union/professional fees		
Subscriptions		
Mortgage/Rent		
Community charge		
Insurance:		
Life		
Household		
Car		
Other		
Heating/lighting		
Hire purchase/loans		
Rentals (TV etc)		
Food		
Household essentials		
Domestic help		
Telephone		
Travel-daily		
Car		
Public transport		
Other		
Car/Vehicle		
Tax		
Repair		
Depreciation		
Child care		
School fees		
University fees		
Covenants (children, grandchildren)		
Newspapers/magazines		
Entertainment		
Eating out		
Guests at home		
Holidays		
Special interests		
Pets		
Cleaning repairs		
Personal		
Household		
Health care		
Postage		
Savings		
Smoking/alcohol		
Gifts		
Special occasions		
Christmas		
Birthdays		
Other		
Other items		
	TOTAL..................	TOTAL..................

EXERCISE 2

BALANCING MY LIFE: NEEDS VERSUS WANTS

You can analyse the difference between what you *think* you want and your true needs by answering questions which demonstrate the benefits and penalties.

What To Do: Complete the sentence 'I want. . . .' e.g. I want more income than I will have if I leave my job. Then write the sentence again, in greater detail e.g. I want to earn some cash, so I'll get another job.

Then answer the following questions. Give at least two responses to each question.

I want ....

Why? ....

What happens if I don't have it? ....

What could I have instead? ....

What do I *really* want? ....

What would I be giving up if I don't have it? ....

What would I gain by doing something else? ....

WHAT DECISIONS WILL I MAKE? ....

EXAMPLE

1 - Miriam

I WANT: More income than I will have if I take voluntary severence.
To earn some cash by getting another job.

WHY:
1 We need another £25 a week to keep up our standard of living.
2 I don't want to give up going to theatres or buying books whenever I want.
3 I don't really want to be at home all day.
4 I'm bored and will miss people, especially the younger trainees.

WHAT HAPPENS IF I DON'T HAVE IT?

1 I'll worry about the money, and feel guilty.
2 I'll become obsessed with housework again!
3 We'll go to the theatre less often, and I'll resent that.

WHAT COULD I HAVE INSTEAD?

1 A part-time job, earning about £30 weekly.
2 Help at the youth club – they pay expenses, and I'd be with young people.
3 Run a secondhand bookstall.
4 Join a class – theatre appreciation – often get cheaper seats.
5 Borrow from the library – go to secondhand bookshops, jumble sales.

WHAT DO I REALLY WANT?

1 A little more money.
2 To feel useful and stimulated.
3 To keep going to the theatre as long as possible.
4 To get hold of the books I want to read.

WHAT WOULD I BE GIVING UP IF I DON'T HAVE IT?

1 Security of having spare cash and entertainment.
2 Being a useful person – interesting to talk to.
3 Company of mixed age groups.
4 Instant gratification with new books.

WHAT WOULD I GAIN BY DOING SOMETHING ELSE?

1 A sense of doing something worthwhile if I work with the youth club – would still feel useful and involved with younger people.
2 More free time – and perhaps still go to theatres, but with cheaper tickets.
3 New interests, skills – and friendship with bookstall staff.

WHAT DECISIONS WILL I MAKE?

Look for a part-time job.
Go and see the Youth worker.
Find out about local Adult Education classes.

EXAMPLE

2 - James

I WANT: To be able to afford steaks regularly.
To enjoy my meals and spend as much on good food as I do now.

WHY:
1 Because meat contains protein and is good for you.
2 Because I've always eaten lots of business meals.
3 Because cheap food takes more effort to cook!
4 Because I enjoy the pleasures of eating out.

WHAT HAPPENS IF I DON'T HAVE IT?

1 I won't enjoy my food so much.
2 I'll get fat – if I change to pasta or potatoes.
3 I'll feel poor, steak is a sign of being well off in my family.
4 I won't think I've eaten properly.

WHAT COULD I HAVE INSTEAD?

1 I could read about food values and see what else would keep me healthy and slim.
2 I could try eating other kinds of meat, or different forms of protein.

WHAT DO I REALLY WANT?

1 I think I'm scared to change lifetime habits, so I want to be safe with everything as it was.
2 I want to eat without having to think about it – and without having to add up the bill every time I shop.
3 I want to stay healthy.
4 I want the status of expense account meals.

WHAT WOULD I BE GIVING UP IF I DON'T HAVE IT?

1 Anxiety about my housekeeping budget!
2 Lifetime habits.
3 If I can believe the nutritionists, steak may not be very good for my health after all.
4 Laziness; I would have to find healthier ways to eat for less money.
5 Possibly a status symbol.

WHAT WOULD I GAIN BY DOING SOMETHING ELSE?

1 Weight, possibly!
2 A more varied diet.
3 Smugness, if I eat better foods and take trouble.

WHAT DECISIONS WILL I MAKE?

Keep steak for special treats and try to enjoy cheaper food.
Find out what is healthy and slimming.
Stop thinking that my lifestyle matters to others.

Miriam and James each found that the 'wants' and the decisions they finally made related to their feelings about losing their present roles. You will need to consider all these factors when facing your new decisions.

Why are more people facing career decisions in their 40's?

Here are some reasons, what might yours be?

1 *My job has changed – in fact it has almost vanished.*
2 *All these computers – can't get the hang of them – prefer people.*
3 *I've been offered freelance work – I'll have a bigger income in the end.*
4 *It's never been the same since the company was taken over.*
5 *I've been ill and want to live a bit longer.*
6 *We've planned for two years – our future is very clearly mapped out.*
7 *There are more prospects if I go full-time.*
8 *The children are older – I can take up my career again.*
9 *They are encouraging re-training.*
10 *They haven't given me much option.*

The next exercise contains trigger sentences to enable you to explore your feelings about mid-life decisions. Completing the sentences may perhaps trigger strong feelings. It may be the first time you have given any deep thought to the implications for you and others of any major changes you make. If possible, discuss the results of the exercise with someone else who is completing it.

EXERCISE 3

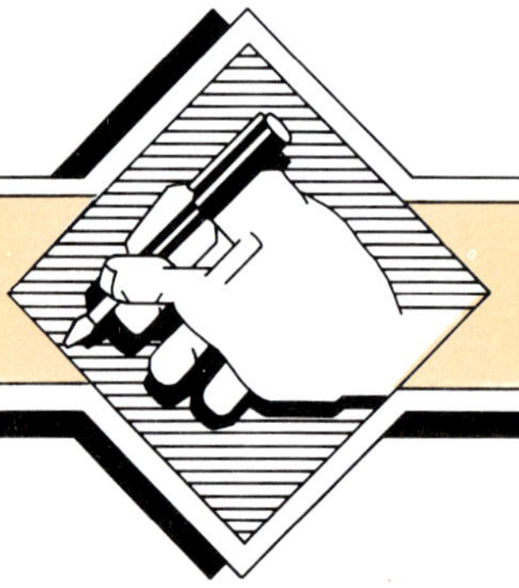

REFLECTIONS ON A LIFE/CAREER CHANGE

What To Do Next: Complete each sentence. The spontaneous response is often the most appropriate, but you may prefer to take time to reflect before writing.

1 I started to think about changing my role when ....

....

2 The biggest challenge I face is ....

....

3 I intend to ....

....

4 I would find it hard to accept losing ....

....

5 I certainly won't miss ....

....

6 The family's reaction to my views is ....

....

7 Other people's reactions have been ....

....

8 If I feel at all worried, I will ....

....

9 Looking back, my life recently has been ....

....

10 When I first started work I ....

....

11 I never thought I'd ....

....

12 My greatest regret is ....

....

13 I have always wanted to ....

....

14 The next six months will ....

....

15 The best thing about the next five years will be ....

....

16 In ten years time, I ....

....

17 Changes always ....

....

18 I need to find out ....

....

What To Do Next: You probably found some of the sentences easier to complete than others. Some answers are more complex than you thought. Your answers to the questions below will indicate where you have the most doubts, and which parts of the book will be most valuable to you.

1 Which sentences were easiest to complete? ....

....

....

2 What surprised you most? ....

....

....

3 Which was the most difficult sentence to complete – why was this? ....

....

....

....

4 What new thoughts about change has this exercise given you? ....

....

....

....

Michael – 51

1 Easiest sentence?
No 13 – I have always wanted to spend much more time carving wood; if I retire early I'll be able to afford to, I might even make some spare cash! I would also say 6, because my family is encouraging me.

2 What surprised me most?
How difficult it was to answer some of the questions, and how much more complicated the decision is than I thought. I was also surprised to find that I was quite upset.

3 Most difficult sentence – and why?
Numbers 11 and 12 – I didn't like admitting, even to myself, that I have regrets about my job. I didn't achieve as much as I'd expected, and I suppose I hoped I was indispensible!

4 New thoughts
Many– but particularly that retiring early will be a major upheaval and I feel as though I am running away from the difficulties.

Marjorie (Returning to full-time work)

1 Easiest sentence?
2 – I'm already dealing with guilt and tiredness!

2 What surprised me most?
Realising how vital it is that I get back into a career, not just a little job!

3 Most difficult sentence – and why?
15 – Because I don't know – can't think beyond this year!

4 New thoughts
I feel from my family how selfish I am at times and I'm a bit scared of the implications.

What is he?

What is he?

— A man, of course.

Yes, but what does he do?

— He lives, and is a man.

Oh, quite! But he must work — he must have a job of some sort.

— Why?

Because obviously he's not one of the leisured classes.

— I don't know. He has lots of leisure.

And he makes quite beautiful chairs.

There you are then! He's a cabinet-maker.

— No, no!

Anyhow, a carpenter and joiner.

— Not at all.

But you said so.

— What did I say?

That he made chairs, and was a joiner and carpenter.

— I said he made chairs, but I did not say he was a carpenter.

All right, then, he's just an amateur.

— Perhaps! Would you say the thrush was a professional flautist,

or just an amateur?

I'd say it was just a bird.

— And I say he is just a man.

All right. You always did quibble.

D.H. Lawrence

Is paid work the only work?

Too often, people who do not earn money are perceived as less valuable than salaried workers. Men and women who leave paid work, for whatever reason, face similar adjustments, but there is often an implicit assumption that women instinctively possess, enjoy and even prefer the skills of homemaking. Careers have been for men, and progress for women has been slow, but there are signs of change. As the shortage of younger workers increases, through lower birthrates in the seventies, women are already being wooed for training and will have more choices of flexible working patterns and career development, although there is still far to go!

What is motivation? What makes us do anything? If you are making a cup of tea you may be motivated by:

thirst;
the wish to entertain a friend;
the wish to please your manager;
the need to escape boredom!

Abraham Maslow suggested that there is a hierarchy of needs which informs people's lifestyles. There has been extensive research into motivation; Maslow's model seems useful in this context.

If people are starving and homeless, all their energies are directed towards finding food and shelter, with little time or incentive to make friends or search for success. Once their basic needs are satisfied, people are motivated to acquire the means to stay comfortable – skills, relationships, a higher income, a place in the community. Only when they achieve recognition and self-respect can people strive to realise their full potential as human beings. It appears that 'self-actualised' people have both the desire and the ability to determine their own life-patterns, which implies they know what they want those patterns to be!

The choices you face at present may spring from a wish to live exactly as you have always wanted, to fulfil your dreams, be more creative. If you have been forced in some way to change direction – perhaps through ill-health or the disappearance of your job, or a relationship, you may be more preoccupied with your basic 'having' needs. Setbacks can affect self-esteem and cause a temporary descent to a lower step.

MASLOW'S HIERARCHY

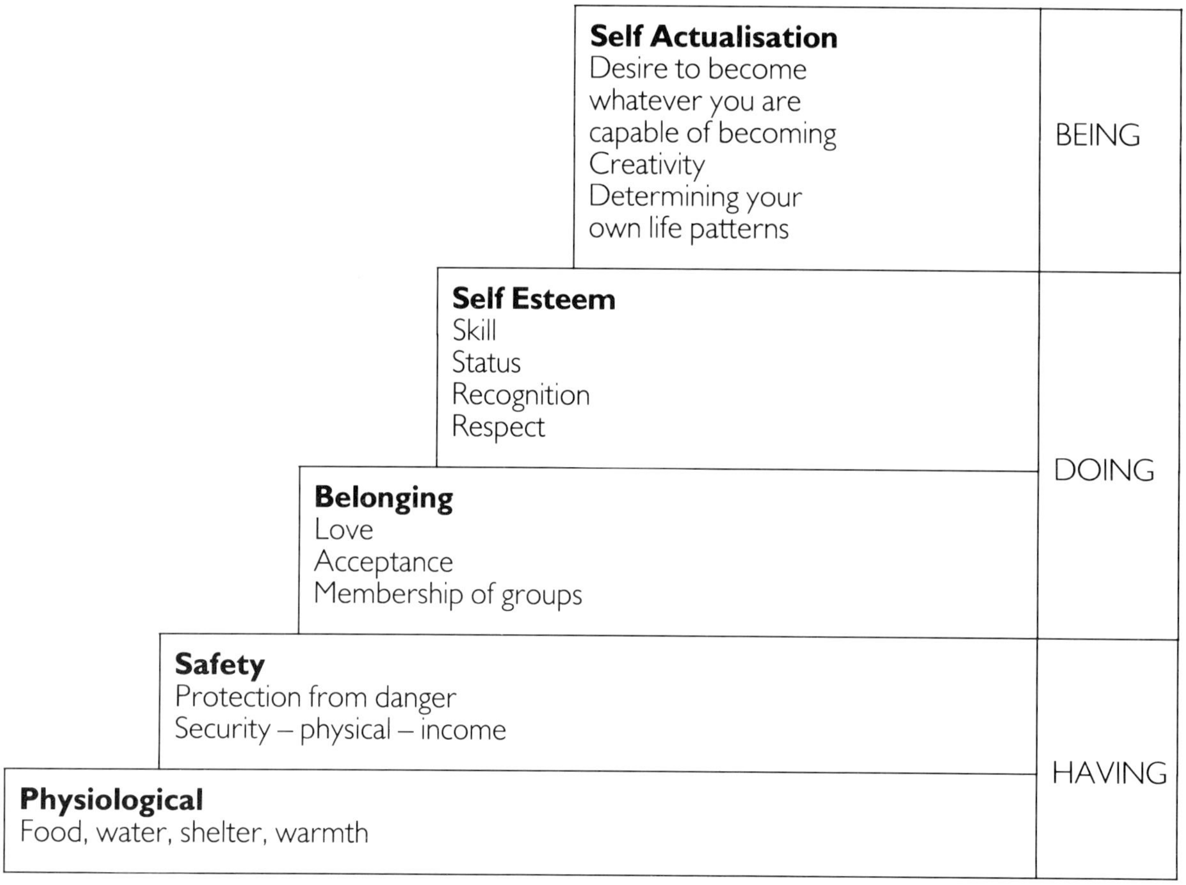

EXERCISE 4

WHAT MOTIVATES ME? WHAT DO I WANT IN THE FUTURE?

What to do: Tick in column 1 those factors which apply to you. Then tick column 2 for those you want to keep. There will probably be some blanks in column 3 which you can fill in as you complete more exercises.

FACTORS IN JOB	FACTORS, IN MY PRESENT JOB	I WANT TO KEEP (OR TO INCLUDE)	HOW CAN I FIND THEM IN FUTURE?
Accommodation (living in)			
Applause – praise			
Base (similar to territory)			
Being needed			
Being of service			
Boredom			
Challenge			
Companionship			
Colleagues			
Contact with the public			
Contact with people with same skills			
Creativity			
Deadlines			
Disappointment			
Discipline			
Exercise			
Feedback			
Frustration			
Identity			
Income			
Independence			
Job satisfaction			
Knowledge			
Mental exertion			
Motivation			
Perks			
Physical exertion			
Physical strength			
Privacy			
Regular meals			
Role			
Routine			
Security			
Sense of belonging			
Sense of purpose			
Skills			
Social life			
Status			
Stress			
Structure of time			
Support			

FACTORS IN JOB	FACTORS, IN MY PRESENT JOB	I WANT TO KEEP (OR TO INCLUDE)	HOW CAN I FIND THEM IN FUTURE?
Teamwork			
Territory			
Topics of conversation			
Travel (to work)			
Travel (in my work)			
Travel (worldwide)			
Vehicle			
Worry			
Younger people to work with			
Other			

Exercise and meals may seem irrelevant to you. Remember the regular walk to the station, or the number of corridors you walk down each day!

If you are considering self-employment, do recognise the importance of 'perks'. They may include typing and other office facilities; storage; tools; transport and other items you may take for granted.

What to do next: Analyse your lists – there may be gaps in column 3, "How can I find them in future?". You will be able to return to this column as you progress through the book.

Make a note of those factors you want to eliminate from your future.

EXAMPLE

Diane

Diane – Training Officer (leaving training role to become freelance)

Factors I want to retain

All 'people' elements
Being needed
Applause
Feedback
Challenge
Independence
Income
Skills
Job satisfaction
Territory
Travel
Exercise

Where can I find the factors I need?

Freelance work will cover all except territory
Friends
New co-trainers
Convert space – room at home
Cycle, Yoga
Plan to work
Hotels with health centres!
I'm excited, not anxious at all, but I know I like to be with people!

PROGRESS SUMMARY

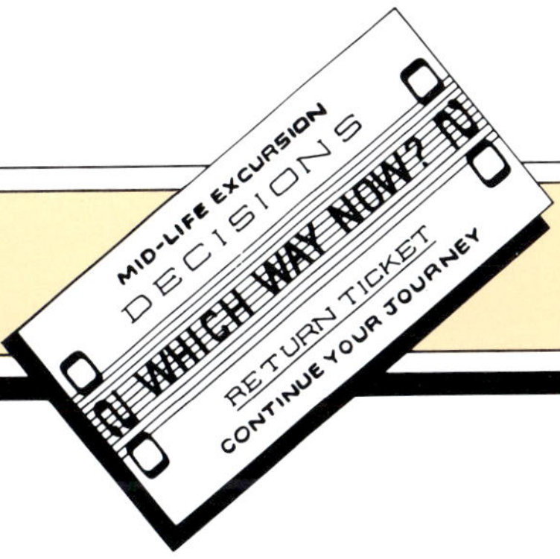

ANALYSIS AND REVIEW OF:

My budget now and in the future.
What I really want.
Feelings about my decisions.
Motivation – self actualisation.
Satisfying factors at work.

IMPORTANT INSIGHTS!

I WANT TO CHANGE:

I WANT TO CONTINUE:

I WANT TO BEGIN, OR TO DEVELOP:

NEW FACTS:

LINKS WITH OTHER PAGES:

WHAT'S NEXT? ON TO:

Managing Change. . . . .

CHAPTER 3

THE MANAGEMENT OF CHANGE

CAN I HANDLE CHANGE?

HOW WILL I COPE WITH THE CHANGES MY LIFE MAY BRING?

HOW HAVE CHANGES AFFECTED ME IN THE PAST?

This chapter explains how people are affected by changes in their lives and how to recognise the normal stages in the adjustment from one situation to another.
Transitions or life changes entail a major readjustment and it is important to understand how you are likely to react.

> *All changes, even the most longed for, have their melancholy for what we leave behind us is a part of ourselves, we must die to one life before we can enter another.*

Anatole France

What are life-changes?

Life-changes are specific events which range from the most painful, like divorce or bereavement, to the very positive – marriage, or becoming a parent. Events related less directly to relationships but which are still major changes, or life crises, include moving house; promotion at work; getting or losing a job; returning to work after raising a family; leaving home, and retirement from paid work. Each of these is a situation which entails adjusting to different norms and ways of behaving. Although the trauma of bereavement is hardly comparable with choosing to leave a job, there are certain predictable patterns in the ways people react to transitions from one way of life to another, which is a simple definition of a life crisis.

The following two exercises and information will enable you:

- to learn what to do to encourage healthy, more rapid adjustment to change;
- to list the transitions you have already experienced;
- to analyse their influences, so that you can understand and predict the way you might react to future significant life changes;
- to understand the stages in the process of transition;
- to recognise specific behaviours which may be linked to events in the past;
- to discover what strategies you use, or can learn, to help you cope with potentially stressful situations.

What might make transitional life changes easier to manage?

- where the change is truly voluntary and has been predicted;
- where other changes are kept to a minimum;
- where there are supportive relationships;
- where self-esteem and confidence are high;
- where there are many interests outside the job;
- where the employing organisation offers opportunities for gradual change;
- where there are firm opportunities to exchange one job for another;
- where employees are offered formal opportunities to plan and explore all their future options.

How many of these factors were present when you thought about changing your circumstances? The longer your list, the more easily you are likely to manage the adjustment. As you focus in depth, first on an important event in your past, and then on your proposed transition, you will be able to list the skills you already have, seen where you need to develop further resources, and ensure you are fully aware of the steps needed to negotiate the Transition.

Exercise 5 will enable you to analyse:

- how many major transitions you have experienced;
- where they happened (at what ages, and what intervals);
- how important they were in your life.

EXERCISE 5 MY TRANSITIONS LIFELINE

You will need to set aside at least half an hour. If possible, try to complete the exercise with a partner – preferably someone else who is working through the book, so that you can listen to each other in turn, as you recall the past, and help each other to recognise factors you may not notice by yourself.

What to do: On a large sheet of paper, draw a line and mark all the important transitions you can remember.

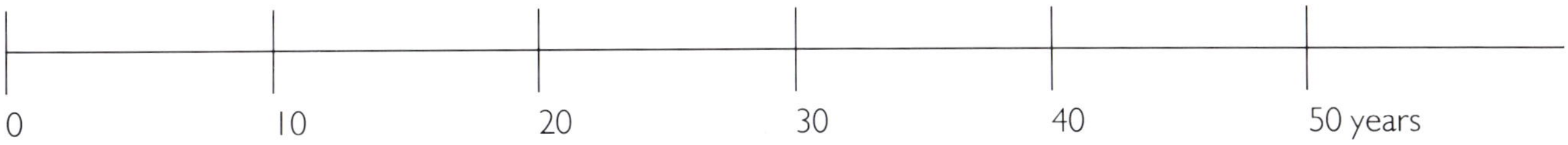

Examples (You can include others which were significant to you.)
Birth – siblings; children; grandchildren; non-births.
Marriage or long-term relationships – beginning and ending.
Becoming a parent – step parent – in-law – children leaving home.
Loss of parent or other close relative – through death or absence.
Major illness – hospital – accidents.
Schools – college – getting qualifications.
Work – getting and changing jobs, unemployment, returning to work.
Leaving home – moving house – going abroad.

Mark EACH transition – e.g. every time you changed school, etc (See John's and Joan's examples on page 29).

What to do next: Study your transitions lifeline and answer these questions:

1 How many transitions have you marked? ....

....

2 Were they concentrated at any one time, spread over intervals, or a mixture? ....

....

3 Which transitions do you feel positive about? ....

....

4 Which ones were upsetting? ....

....

5 How did you react to the lifeline as you reflected on the transitions? ....

....

6 Did anything surprise you? ....

....

7 What was your most interesting discovery? ....

....

EXAMPLE

Joan - Sales Manager

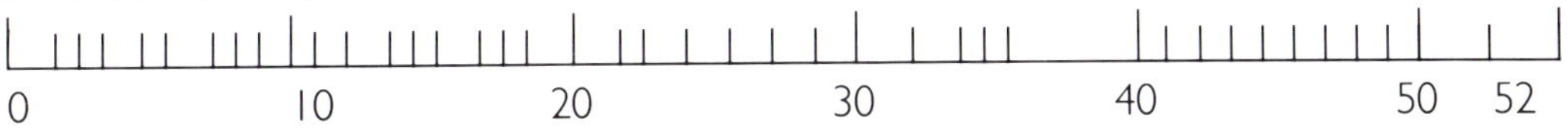

1 *I put 37, although there would be many more if I had counted all the times my husband worked away from home for long periods, and minor illnesses.*
2 *Before 20, and 40-48. My 30's seem very uneventful, but it was my most satisfying time!*
3 *Having my children; going back to work at 42 and making a success of it; the early years of my marriage.*
4 *After I went back to work, the next five years were awful. Both my parents died, my marriage broke up; one of my daughters got pregnant and then miscarried. I was too depressed to go to work, but was unaware how much these events had upset me. My arthritis began suddenly, when I was 46.*
5 *I felt upset and was surprised how irritable I got. Almost gave up the exercise, but my friend was very sympathetic.*
6 *I was surprised to realise how all the moves I had as a child must have affected my need to stay put now. I have few memories, except of being almost constantly on the move – there was never time to make any friends. I have moved house only once since my marriage. When I went to University I had to leave through illness, and I was always changing jobs. One of the reasons my husband left was my refusal to travel with him; he also said I kept too quiet about my feelings.*
7 *Most interesting discovery? I find it difficult to accept, yet it seems to make sense – I have been dreading another house move, although I made the decision very carefully; that seems obvious link with my past. I wonder if this means I shouldn't move? I'll see what the rest of this chapter has to say!*

EXAMPLE

John - Production Manager
Agricultural Machinery

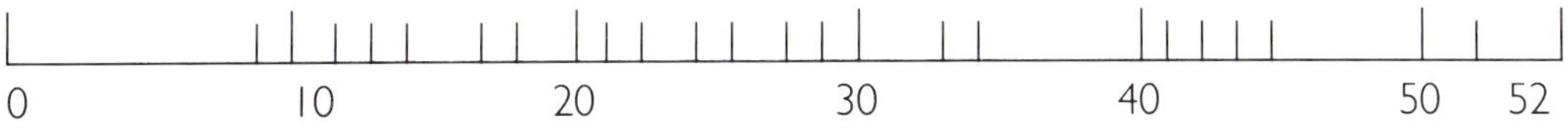

1 *19. I appear to have lived a very uneventful life. I am an only child who lived in the country, and left home when I was married.*
2 *14-28. All I did before I was 10 was to go to the local school!*
3 *My marriage, my promotions at work.*
4 *Although I hated National Service, leaving it and the friends I made there; I keep remembering it now – changing jobs was upsetting – leaving the team behind.*
5 *I felt quite uncomfortable, and amused by my comparatively short list.*
6 *Not exactly surprised, but I now see that there is a link between leaving National Service and changing my job – perhaps that's why it keeps coming into my mind.*
7 *Most interesting discovery – that all my major traumas have still to come. I've no idea how I will cope when my parents die, but I'm a pretty calm person.*

Joan and John had very different transition lifelines. Joan recognised how her earlier experiences and one job change affected her attitudes in adult life. John, apart from his National Service had comparatively few changes. By exploring further, they each discovered more about their likely reactions to change and began to see patterns in the ways they coped with changes.

Focusing on the pattern – helping to ease the transition

By exploring one important event in your past in depth you can begin to build a picture of the resources you already have and to see where you want to develop more.

EXERCISE 6

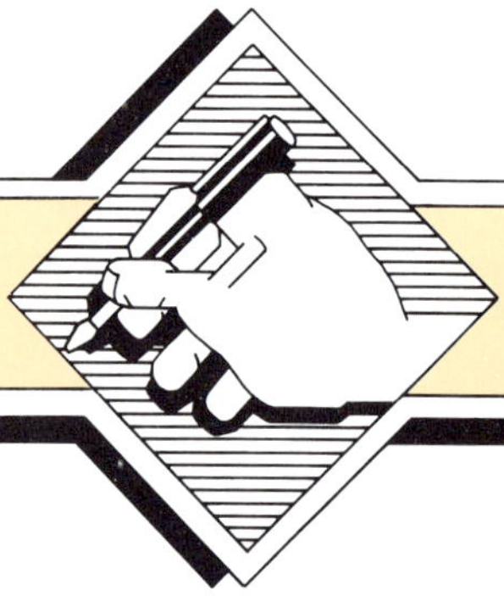

TRANSITION MANAGEMENT PATTERNS – PAST AND PRESENT

This exercise is in three stages.
Stage I:
What to do: Choose an important life-change and write it down here.

....

....

Answer the following questions about it:

1 Did you know it was going to happen?

....

2 Do you remember how you felt when it happened?

....

3 Did anyone help you?

....

4 Was there anyone to talk to?

....

5 Could you have done anything to make it easier?

....

6 Did you have to look for support, or was it already there?

....

7 Did you want this transition?

....

8 If you were alone, could you have found someone if necessary?

....

9 Could you have changed the situation?

....

10 What did you learn from the transition?

....

EXAMPLE

John

He was uncertain whether to choose his first day at school, or his daughter's wedding. He chose the latter.

1 *Yes, of course I knew – I had to finance it.*
2 *A mixture of shock and resentment – I found it hard to believe my baby was grown up enough to marry!*
3 *Not really. My wife tried to. She teased me when I tried to tell her Jane was too young – said I was jealous. It wasn't funny at the time.*
4 *Not really – I find it difficult to talk about myself, especially if I'm not being taken seriously.*
5 *Just had to grin and bear it.*
6 *Jane kept asking if I was OK; I pretended I was as I didn't want to worry her. I suppose she could have reassured me.*
7 *Yes and No. Reminds me time is passing and that she's someone else's.*
8 *There were times when I nearly talked to my colleague as his daughter lived with her boyfriend, but I felt stupid.*
9 *No. Well, perhaps not the wedding, but my worries.*
10 *Letting go is very difficult.*

If John had chosen his first day at school, some of his answers would obviously have been very different, but the general theme, of keeping his worries to himself, would have probably have been the same. When he answered the next set of questions, John revealed more of his feelings.

What To Do Next: Talk to somebody about your answers and see if you recognise any themes in your response to changes.

Stage 2:
Please use the same event as in Stage 1.

1 After the event happened, what did you miss most?

....

2 What were you glad to lose?

....

3 What did you keep – memories, skills, knowledge, possessions, etc?

....

4 What were your feelings after it happened?

....

5 What were your first thoughts?

....

6 Who did you meet – what did they say to you?

....

7 Were you well-prepared ?

....

8 What would you have liked to know?

....

9 What did other people expect of you?

....

10 How did you respond to their expectations?

....

11 What did you want from other people?

....

12 Did you let them know?

....

13 What did you enjoy about the change?

....

14 What was least enjoyable?

....

15 Looking back, are your memories of the event and the time before it: pleasant; wistful; angry; resentful, sad; other?

....

EXAMPLE

John

Jane's Wedding

1	*I missed having her around the house; even though she had spent most of the time with Richard, she still lived* at home.
2	*I suppose I was glad to lose my anxiety when she came home late (my wife says it was the large phone bills!).*
3	*I have all my memories of her childhood, some of her books and toys.*
4	*I admit I secretly hoped Richard wouldn't turn up. Not seriously, I suppose I was jealous. I had quite a lump in my throat and couldn't eat all day; felt a bit of a fool, really, I was behaving as though she'd gone forever.*
5	*I couldn't believe a ten-minute ceremony could turn her into a different person, yet I thought things would never be the same again.*
6	*All the guests kept saying things like 'You're gaining a son' or 'Peace and quiet at last' – I felt very irritated, they didn't understand.*
7	*Thought I was – I had no idea I'd be so upset.*
8	*Follows on – wish I'd known most fathers feel like this, I felt quite guilty.*
9	*Wanted me to be cheerful – I was, on the surface. My wife got quite embarrassed.*
10	*Kept a fixed grin. I apologised to my wife.*
11	*To shut up or commiserate – pretty unreasonable of me.*
12	*No you don't make a fuss about things like that.*
13	*It was a wonderful day. She had a lovely time and now I can look back with pleasure – I'm very fond of Richard.*
14	*My own irrational and stupid reaction.*
15	*All of those, plus guilt and irritation.*

John saw that his replies, even though they were humourous, reinforced his need to keep his feelings to himself – and his feelings of guilt.

Spend some time thinking about and discussing *your* discoveries. Then think about the current transition you have already made or have yet to confront. The final set of questions will focus your thoughts on the most crucial aspects of the transition. The two sets of questions are very alike and will help you clarify the relevance of your patterns to any transitions you make.

Transition Patterns

Stage 3:
My mid-life transition

1 When did you realise you needed to make a decision?

....

2 Did you suggest it, or were you told about it?

....

3 How did you feel immediately after you knew?

....

4 How did you feel two or three days later?

....

5 What did you do first?

....

6 What are the most pleasing aspects of the change?

....

7 What are the less pleasant factors?

....

8 What have you done to help yourself manage this change?

....

9 What has anyone else done for you?

....

10 Could you have had more help?

....

11 How could you find that help?

....

12 How will your analysis of your transition patterns influence your future development?

....

13 What other transitions have happened over the past 5 years?

....

14 Do you know of other transitions which are likely to happen soon?

....

EXAMPLE

John

My decision to relocate with the company

1 *Rumours have been around for a year – definite invitation last week.*
2 *Bit of both – I went to ask what the position was. He gave me total freedom to decide.*
3 *In a whirl – wanted to phone my wife and tell her.*
4 *Mixed – excited, quite cross, annoyed at the disruption, apprehensive about making new friends.*
5 *Rearranged my office . . . . . no idea why.*
6 *Generous relocation assistance and knowing the company values me.*
7 *I've always lived here so I shall miss it all*
8 *Talked to my wife. Done my sums. Thought a lot.*
9 *Plenty of people to give me advice, but it is confusing.*
10 *Don't know. I could talk to my brother-in-law, as he left the company last year.*
11 *Ring and invite him for a drink but I don't want to bother him.*
12 *It reinforced my reluctance to discuss my personal problems, but I have promised my wife that I will ring my brother-in-law and another colleague who moved two years ago. We have found this exercise very helpful.*

You may find it useful at this stage to complete an interim progress summary:

INTERIM

PROGRESS SUMMARY

I have learned that when major changes happen in my life, I am likely to:

....

....

Events in my life which have influenced me are:

....

....

To help me face transitions confidently I need to:

....

....

Understanding the Transition Process: General Stages: Normal Reactions

> *Every change involves a loss and a gain. The old environment must be given up, the new accepted. People come and go; one job is lost, another begun; territory and possessions are accrued or sold; new skills are learned, old abandoned; expectations are fulfilled or hopes dashed. In all these situations the individual is faced with the need to give up one mode of life and accept another.*
>
> C Murray Parkes

It is not possible to predict exactly how someone will react, as every experience is influenced by many different variables. There is, however, a distinct and recognisable pattern in the stages of transition. The type and depth of event will obviously affect the strength of the reaction and the time taken to complete the process – promotion is more welcome than redundancy; marriage more positive than divorce. Bereavement is the greatest trauma, and it is normal to take two years to recover from a major bereavement.

The transition curve below shows a typical response to a major decision, in this case the decision to accept voluntary redundancy. See if you recognise in it your own reactions to the change you are facing and the transitions you have just explored.

Some of these reactions will be more or less acute depending on the nature of the charge. Even welcome changes are often accompanied by phases of doubt, nostalgia for the old situation and regret, anxiety or uncertainty about what the new situation will bring.

The Transition Curve – reactions to voluntary redundancy

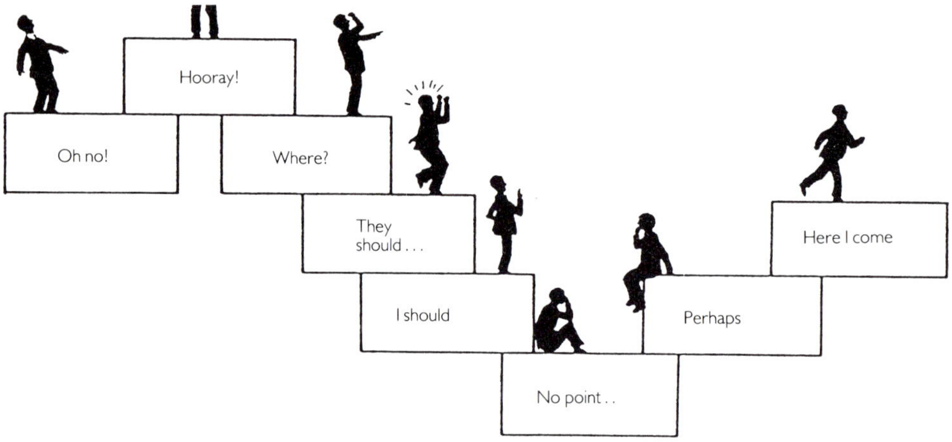

Shock, denial:	Unable to understand, to believe it has happened. 'You're joking! . . .' 'I couldn't take it in'. Sometimes frantic, useless activity.
Euphoria, minimising:	Making the best of it. Everything to look forward to – paint the house, do the garden, take a holiday, spend money – didn't like the job anyway.
Pining, searching:	Going back; hallucinations, sometimes bad dreams.
Anger:	Blame someone – the company, the Government, the victim . . . They should have . . .
Guilt:	Blame the self . .'If only I'd . . .' 'It's my fault, I chose it . . .'
Depression, despair, apathy:	Powerless, lack of motivation . . . to get up, to plan, to do anything new. At its worst, too much effort to stay alive.
Gradual acceptance:	Letting go – taking up old activities, starting new ones; new energy.

- The process has no definite time-span.
- It can last from two minutes to many years.
- Each stage may be very brief, and tends to recur.

For some people the transition curve lasts only a few days; others have felt upset for much longer. They also report feelings of guilt, simply because they had chosen to make the change and then became dissatisfied with their choice.

Depression covers all the shades of feeling low, ranging from boredom and irritation to a real inability to see anything postitive ahead. The feeling may affect others who are involved and they may show signs of strain.

Being angry with the victim, implies that it is often difficult to be sympathetic, or to offer unending encouragement. Easy to blame – 'It's your own fault, you chose it'. Unfortunately, depression is infectious. Anger with the victim of an accident or with someone who has died, is also difficult to comprehend. It takes the form of resenting being left behind, or of thinking briefly 'They should have been more careful'. There is nothing wrong or abnormal about such anger, but it is often difficult to acknowledge.

It is normal or even healthy to experience these feelings briefly

If you cannot recognise any of the parts of the transition curve, test whether it works for you at a simple level. Remember the last time you lost your keys – or the cat. How many times did you search your bag and other hiding places? Were you angry with them for 'getting lost'... or did you feel depressed by your own incompetence? All these different reactions in the space of half a minute and in walks the cat!

Who Might Take Longer To Adjust?

Many people do not feel they have made a free choice. For this group an understandable anger and guilt may persist. Family support will help the adjustment, but some people lack close relationships, and may become very isolated if they have no-one with whom they can discuss their anxieties.

Recognising the symptoms

Accepting and talking about the negative and upsetting feelings is one way to let go of them. One woman said she went through most of the reactions on the transition curve in one awful day, two months after she had happily retired early. She recalled her 'Searching'. She had almost telephoned her former colleagues to beg them for a few hours work! Others report being irritable, having headaches or colds, being tempted to eat or drink more than usual; altered sleeping patterns (waking early, or sleeping much longer than usual). Addiction to television, or excuses to avoid going out are all minor symptoms of a slight disturbance in emotional balance, and quite *normal* – even healthy.

If you are at all concerned about your behaviour, or that of others around you, do find someone to talk to if possible. Perhaps you have felt depressed for longer than you think is reasonable, or there are other unusual patterns of behaviour. You do not necessarily need a doctor – talking to any sympathetic listener may help.

Strategies for successful survival

In addition to the factors which help adjustment to transitions, there are ways of making sure you are prepared to cope with stressful situations.

Rituals help us to face reality

Many mixed emotions accompany the process of winding down, tying up loose ends, and letting go of the old situation. Saying 'Goodbye', formally or informally, can be upsetting. Many people try to avoid formal farewells, yet the rituals are important, as they symbolise the reality of the event. Those staying behind may feel upset but try not to 'spoil' things, and there is often an air of false jollity – another sign of the 'stiff upper lip' culture which refuses to acknowledge pain! As the farewell rituals end, the real negotiation of the transition has begun.

Importance of negotiating the transition

Does it matter if you don't show that you are upset, or if you never get the resentment? Unfortunately, unresolved grief, for this is what we are talking about, can lead to illness, both physical and mental.
If you deny that something has happened, how can you begin to deal with it? Peter Nixon, a cardiologist at Charing Cross Hospital, quotes a German study of men who suffered heart attacks. There was a high incidence of unresolved life crises. It seems although many of the patients had a high level of physical fitness (including exercise, diet, smoking, etc.), psychological risk factors were highly influential as causes of cardiac disease; there is a growing body of evidence which indicates that many illnesses have their roots in unresolved and unacknowledged personal life crises. The body is more vulnerable to infection in periods of distress.

There is further discussion of the link between stress and ill health in Chapter 8: Do I Take Care of Myself?

Basic Survival Strategies

- Get as much information as possible about the new situation.
- Know yourself – how you react; how you make decisions; how you relax.
- List all the useful people you know – a network for support, for fun, for closeness and to give you information.
- Take care of yourself and your body.
- Express your feelings – use anger constructively; keep the best memories, but live in the present and let go of the past.
- Set yourself new goals; make decisions; look for alternatives to replace what is missing.
- Practise relaxation and deep breathing; become calm (not rigid!).

These strategies may seem obvious – and yet are difficult to practise if you are feeling low.
This chapter has been about transitions, or life crises. The Chinese symbol for crisis is Wei Chi, meaning Danger – Opportunity. Transition management is about recognising the dangers and seizing the opportunities!

危 危 机

险 机 会

As you progress through the book, and discover all the possibilities open to you, you are developing the tools to set objectives and prepare for the future – moving through the 'Danger' to the 'Opportunity'.
You will at times be confused, feeling as though you are on a seesaw.

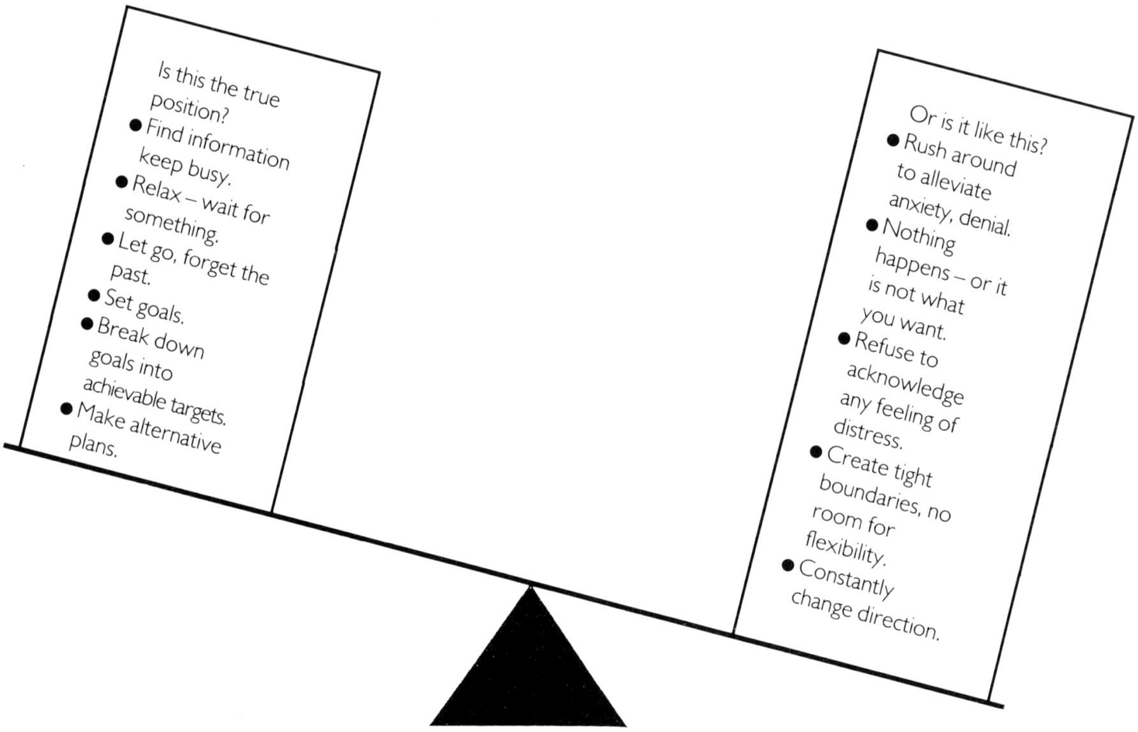

This is a wide range of opportunities, but now your euphoria may have vanished, and already you are wondering how you will fill your time. It is important to remember that doubt and fluctuating emotions are normal.

PROGRESS 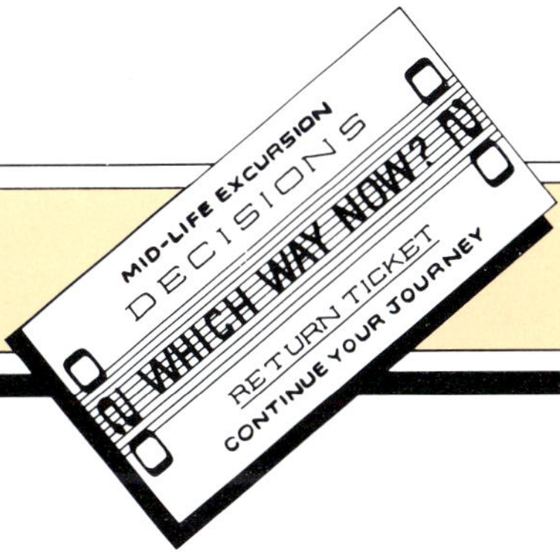 SUMMARY

ANALYSIS AND REVIEW OF:

Factors enabling the management of change.

The transition process.
Personal transition patterns.
Problems in adjusting – strategies for survival.

IMPORTANT INSIGHTS:

I WANT TO CHANGE:

I WANT TO CONTINUE:

I WANT TO BEGIN, OR TO DEVELOP:

NEW FACTS:

LINKS WITH OTHER PAGES:

WHAT'S NEXT? ON TO:
Making the most of the middle years – what else is happening in your life?
– what plans might you need to make?

CHAPTER 4

THE MIDDLE YEARS: MAKING THE MOST OF THEM

HOW MAY I BE AFFECTED BY OUTSIDE EVENTS?

HOW AM I AFFECTED BY THE MYTHS OF AGEING?

HOW CAN I MINIMISE STRESS CAUSED BY THESE FACTORS?

This chapter examines new patterns of employment and changes in the age distribution of the population. The middle years are a time of transition in family life and there is an exercise which will enable you to predict how many outside events are likely to affect you over the next few years, so you can take steps to minimise any stress which may arise from too many transitions happening together.

Stocktaking – changes in society

> *Powerful trends are combing to create a breakdown in existing values, existing lifestyles and existing instructions.*

James Robertson: The Sane Alternative.

There are many myths about ageing; the myths are examined and challenged, with facts about physiological development and an excercise, 'The Ages of Me', which offers an opportunity to demolish some of your personal myths! The chapter ends with a description of adult lifestages and proposes new definitions which may be needed as we prepare to enter a new century. By the end of the chapter you will be able to see what changes will affect your middle years, as you begin this new phase of your life.

When you began your first job, if you thought about it at all you probably envisaged spending most of your working life in one organisation, or taking a break to rear a family, possibly returning to work part-time.

Work patterns fitted the 48 x 3 rule
48 hours – for 48 weeks – for 48 years

This pattern is unlikely to return – it begins to look more like 35 x 3, and those 35 years may not be consecutive, but will include breaks for study, for sabbaticals, for retraining and for non-paid employment. The pace of change in the world of work is rapid; it is exciting but also confusing. Young people will probably change direction two or three times during their lives. The length of a working lifetime varies with the demands of the economy and the age distribution of the population. Since the seventies, the shortage of jobs for young people and the radical contraction of many industries popularised the idea of retirement at 50. The children of the 'baby boom' years are now adult; there are too few young people entering the job market and ever-increasing numbers of healthy over-50s. Already there are rumours of encouragement to work, at least part-time, until 70, and efforts to recruit and retrain women! The situation poses many interesting questions which may be relevant to the choices you face.

Personal Events In The Middle Years

What is happening in your life which may influence your choices?

In Exercise 6 you saw how early life transitions influence adult attitudes and learned that positive adjustment can depend on the number of changes which happen over a relatively short time. Exercise 7 will enable you to estimate the depth and pace of recent transitions and those which you expect in the next year or so.

If possible, spread out some of the future changes as it may be extremely stressful to experience several major changes at once. If the events are inevitable, or where they have already happened, take steps to acquire stress management skills (Chapter 8).

EXERCISE 7

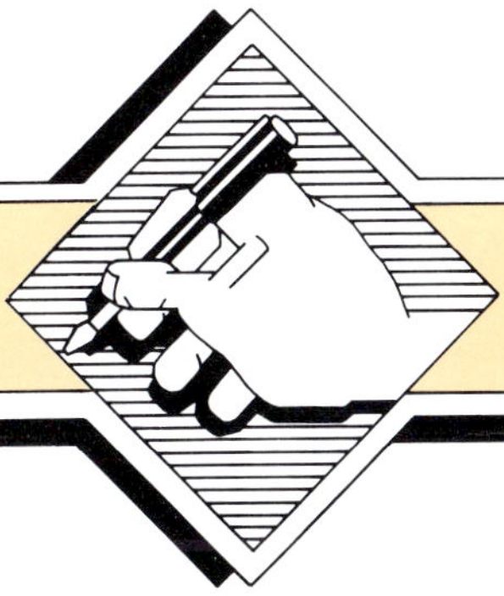

EVENTS OF MY MIDDLE YEARS

This exercise is different from the transitions lifeline. It focuses on a very short period in your life and includes future transitions.

The objective is to highlight the number of transitions affecting both you and your family in the past year, or which are likely to happen in the next year or so, and determine how much pressure this may cause. There is no evaluation of the importance of each transition; everyone reacts differently.

What To Do: Mark each event in the appropriate column(s). Some of them may happen more than once, for instance three children may have left home!

Event	Happened in the past year.	Inevitable in the next year.	Possible in the near future.
In My Life			
1 Becoming a parent or step-parent			
2 Death of partner			
3 Death of relative or close friend			
4 Divorce			
5 Extra-marital relationship			
6 Job change:			
Early retirement			
New job			
Redundancy			
7 Major accident			
8 Marital breakdown			
9 Marriage or re-marriage			
10 Menopause			
11 Moving house			
12 Serious illness			
13 Return to paid work			
In My Partner's Life Some of events 1-13 will also affect my partner			
14 Early retirement			
15 Major illness			
16 New full-time job			
17 New part-time job			
18 Promotion			
19 Redundancy			
20 Retirement			
21 Other			

Event	Happened in the past year.	Inevitable in the next year.	Possible in the near future.
In My Childrens' Lives			
22 Childbirth			
23 Divorce			
24 Leaving home			
25 Marital breakdown			
26 Marriage or long-term partnership			
27 Pregnancy			
28 Starting work			
29 Studying (school or college)			
30 Unemployment			
31 Other			
In My Parents' Lives			
32 Moving into my home			
33 Moving to residential accommodation			
34 Needing care in hospital			
35 Needing care in their home			
36 Other			
TOTAL			

What To Do Next: Add the totals in columns 1, 2 and 3.

Overall total: Up to 12 overall: Normal (unless it is 12 divorces!)

13-20: Manageable; depends on importance of the events; some tension likely.

21+: Accept that you will be under some pressure.

How do you view your total?

Images Of Ageing

Once you are forty, are you on the way down? While some people will be itching to begin new careers, others may perceive themselves as 'on the way to the scrap-heap', no longer regarded as able or useful.

Mid-life, like adolescence, can be a time of confusion and experienced in very different ways. The cliche 'you are as old as you feel' seems to be highly relevant to those who are 40+. Or rather, 'you are as old as other people see you!'

Demolishing Myths

Myth:	. . .Surely not at *your age?* You get tired easily. . .rest more. . .conserve your energy. *You* couldn't run in a marathon.	**Fact:**	The more you exercise a limb, the fitter you become. . . use it or lose it
Myth:	How disgusting – pregnant at 42!	**Fact:**	Older women who become pregnant often feel embarrassment or guilt. Denis Compton, veteran cricketer and a new father at 67, said he thought those who dis-approved were probably jealous!
Myth:	Women's place is in the home. . .	**Fact:**	42% of the workforce is female. 69% of married women have paid jobs.
Myth:	Only the young can pass exams.	**Fact:**	Open University degrees have been gained by several hundred students over 55.
Myth:	We would expect the successful applicant to be under 35.	**Fact:**	Experience and maturity are often more effective than youth.

What about the wear and tear of the years? Surely the body deteriorates when you get older?

Physical ageing – myth and reality

When does this 'ageing' begin? (You may be surprised!)

Physiological Change and Age

After 20	Gradual loss of hearing: sight tends to diminish.
16 – 25	Sexual potency at its peak in adolescence for men – mid-twenties for women!
25 – 33	Strength peaks – manual dexterity greatest – muscles may begin to deteriorate.
20 – 30	Peak of creative output for chemists, mathematicians.
45	Peak for architects.
40 – 50's	Peak for novelists.

Crystallised intelligence (storage of general information and vocabulary) increases over adult years.

When highly motivated, older adults learn new skills, e.g. a language – as quickly as or more quickly than children.

So – your deterioration began at 20!!

There is however one phsyiological change which belongs in the middle years:

The menopause

- Is the menopause a transition of the middle years?
- Isn't it just a health issue?
- Isn't it of interest only to women?

It is arguable that the menopause is a health issue and should be in Chapter 9, but as it is a significant event of the middle years for the majority of women, it has been deliberately included in a discussion of myths about ageing. There is increasing evidence that men, too, experienced menopausal symptons, although they have no physical sign comparable with the cessation of menstruation in women. Because there are still many taboos which make women reluctant to discuss any anxieties or to seek help, the indications of menopause are discussed in some detail.

Menopause – what are the symptoms?

It is difficult to accept the concept of a 'male menopause': it has for so long been a 'woman's problem' – associated with the end of the ability to bear children (and often dismissed as neurosis!). However, there is evidence to suggest that some men experience severe discomfort and inconvenience from very rapid hormonal changes. Many of the symptoms described below affect both men and women; they may be due to the menopause, but may also indicate other stresses.

The menopause may cause:

Fatigue; mood swings; memory lapses; headaches; depressive phases; dizziness; flushing; loss of sexual desire; sweating; anxiety; irritability; sudden irrational rages. Fears of ageing or of failure may be signs of a loss of confidence, or the result of other symptoms. The menopause can continue for many years after the last period.

If you recognise the symptoms described here there is no need to 'grin and bear it'. Too many members of the medical profession still dismiss any attempt to seek help as 'Your age, my dear!'. There are special menopause clinics in many hospitals, or Well Women clinics, which can offer general support as well as, or instead of, hormone replacement therapy.

Now you have explored some of the facts and the myths about ageing, how old do *you* feel?

> *The years beyond 50 are now seen as a potentially rewarding stage of the life-cycle, so the possibility of offering a more flexible work pattern becomes not only feasible, but desirable.*

D Wedderburn

Exercise 8 enables you to see if your outlook is typical of your age group, and how comfortable you are with your developmental age. A section on theories of adult development follows the exercise, and you can determine which 'Stage of Adulthood' is appropriate.

You may decide you fit one of the new categories of the 'Lifestages 2005'!

EXERCISE 8

THE AGES OF ME

What To Do: Fill in the gaps in the following sentences:

1 In other people's eyes I look as though I am about .... years old.
2 In my own eyes, my body is like that of a person about .... years old.
3 My thoughts and interests are like those of a person about .... years old.
4 My role in society is that of a person about .... years old.
5 My relationships are like those of a person about .... years old.
6 Deep inside, I feel like a person about .... years old.
7 I would prefer to be about .... years old.
8 After early retirement, I will feel about .... years old.

What To Do Next: There is no score to this exercise. Read the summary of Stages of Adulthood 1980's and the Stages of Adulthood 2005? next to it on the following page.

Answer the questions:

1 Are you comfortable with your present age?

....

2 Which Lifestage is most appropriate to you?

....

3 Does it match your chronological age?

....

4 Where do you fit in the Stages of Adulthood, 2005?

....

How simple – or useful – is it to define development stages for adults?

For more than three thousand years philosophers have periodically studied the 'ages of man'. The Talmud outlined fourteen stages: in 700BC the poet Solon divided life into ten stages. Confucius, in 500BC identified six. Daniel Lewinson and Gail Sheehy, both Americans, renewed an interest in Adult Life-stages:

> "*The nature of adult life was one of the best-kept secrets of our society.*"

All the world's a stage, and all the men and women merely players:
One man in his time plays many parts, His acts being seven ages.

Shakespeare

STAGES OF ADULTHOOD 1980'S

Provisional Adulthood 20 – 28
First commitments to work, to family and to close relationships – marriage – seeking an adult identity.

Age 30 Transition 28 – 30
Re-examining and questioning earlier commitments. Life seems complex, earlier choices perhaps unwise. Assessment of longer implications of career and relationships. Major change, or affirmation of satisfactions with current lifestyle, community, etc.

Rooting 32 – 39
Life seems more settled after 35; time assumes importance – perhaps first intimations of mortality, undesirable or unrealistic. Upheaval in marriage or lifestyle for some. Many seek a mentor.

Mid-Life Transition 40 – 45
A period often labelled 'Mid-Life Crisis'. Essential to confront the gap between aspirations and reality. Can be a lonely time – children growing up and leaving; parents needing support; questioning marriage and close relationships. Recurrence of upheavals of 32 – 39. Questions concern time – can I still find success? Or fun? What is life about? What purpose?

Restabilisation and flowering 45 – 55
Can be the most stable stage of life, as the mid-life crisis is over. Financial peak – few demands on income. Basic, familiar values and companions important. Illness and death may impinge. Possible return to earlier stages if there are major disruptions. Career at its peak.

Mellowing and Renewal 55 – 65+
Tendency to accept oneself and to live in the present. There may be traumatic reactions to the need to come to terms with retirement and the shift from paid work, plus the likelihood of losing companions. Can be a fruitful and rewarding time. Gradual relaxing into the wisdom of the elder.

STAGES OF ADULTHOOD 2005?

Although the chronological ages were used only as general boundaries, so that a person's outlook could be typical of more than one Stage, or could regress without significant 'immaturity', there are signs of a need for more flexibility in future definitions.

In Gail Sheehy's research* it was emphasised that women's progress through the Life Stages is recognisably different from men's. Increasing dilemmas over child-bearing and rearing mean the Age 30 transition may be postponed to Age 35, and an increasing number of single-parent families, usually female. Because of their family, – men, parents, grandparents – women often begin their mid-life crisis at 45 or so. As we begin slowly to move away from the stereotyped images of women as child-rearers and men as breadwinners the sexes may move closer in their management of their lives.

RELATIONSHIPS
New patterns of relationships – couples living together, hetrosexuality no longer the major norm. High divorce and remarriage rates mean that marriage will not necessarily be so important in the Life Stages and commitments will be made much later. The changes in employment patterns make it likely that Provisional Adulthood may be delayed, or the activities in that stage will change.

*See Chapter 10, Other Resources.

The 46 year old planning a second marriage may think like the 20 – 30 year old. The greatest change will be in the mid-life transition. Mellowing may not begin until after 60 – 65; retirement will no longer be such a trauma – the mid-life transition itself will be leaving full-time employment – for part-time self-employment; craftsmanship; income from pension; leisure lifestyle.

Are The Middle Years Heralding A New Phase Of Life For All? Will The Majority Change Direction At 40+?

As long ago as 1908 Lloyd George was pleading for flexibility of choice in the time to retire from employment.

A former steel worker from Consett expressed considerable distress that at 48 he was filed at the Job Centre as a labourer. There were no more jobs in his own highly skilled specialist field "It's not the money, I just feel I don't count any more".

You have explored the changes that you face, personal and societal, in your middle years, and studied myths and realities about ageing.

PROGRESS SUMMARY

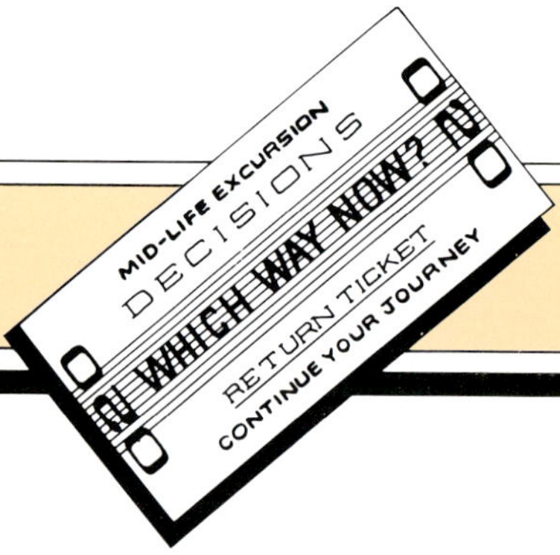

ANALYSIS AND REVIEW OF:

Changes in the world of employment.
Changes in the middle years – Middle Years Catalogue.
Images of ageing – Physiological ageing – Menopause.
The Ages of Me – Lifestages.

IMPORTANT INSIGHTS:

I WANT TO CHANGE:

I WANT TO CONTINUE:

I WANT TO BEGIN, OR TO DEVELOP:

NEW FACTS:

LINKS WITH OTHER PAGES:

WHAT'S NEXT? ON TO:
The people in your life – relationships – where to live?

CHAPTER 5

WHO ELSE IS THERE IN MY LIFE?

WHAT WILL BE THE EFFECT OF MY CHOICES ON OTHER PEOPLE?

WHO WILL BE AFFECTED?

HOW WILL I COPE WITH THIS?

This chapter sets out to help you estimate as accurately as possible who will share your life in the future. There may certainly be contented recluses, but humans are generally social animals: they need others to talk to, to reassure them that they matter, for mutual support and respect, to laugh with and to touch . . . and to argue with. People also need privacy at times, but to be free to choose solitude.

No man is an island entire of itself; every man is a piece of the continent, a part of the main.

John Donne

Many transitions also affect others close to the person who goes through the change. The loss of another person may be central in the transition you face, for example, getting divorced; the youngest child finally leaving home, a close friend or colleague moving away. Your relationships with others may be affected as a result of the transition – redundancy, retirement, returning to work, relocation to another company site – all bring an important shift in old relationships and social networks. They may bring feelings of apprehension about being isolated, or starting afresh, but they also bring opportunities for new social networks and new close relationships too.

The first exercise in this chapter will help you to clarify who will be part of your life, which of your needs they meet, who will be missing from your network, and where you might need to make new contacts.

Different people are important for different aspects of life, and although the same names may recur frequently, make sure you do not rely too heavily on one relationship. It is wonderful to have a partner who is a friend, mentor, lover, carer, but what will you do if that companion disappears from your life?

Like lions, we are meant to live in a social group and we need the support and companionship of our fellow man.

Audrey Livingstone Booth, Stressmanship

I know exactly what is in the bank – my wallet – the deep freeze – my holiday fund.

I must save for my daughter – grandson. Can't have a new coat – holiday – warm house.

There's always been enough in the end – if the meal costs a lot, I'll go without tomorrow – I must cook for my friends.

How will I manage without two cars – two homes – two incomes? How will I face my neighbours?

We pay for everything by monthly Banker's Order – plan essentials, do what we like with the rest.

I'll have to get work – but I'll have problems – don't like to go on state aid. Like to be independent.

EXERCISE 9

MY PERSONAL NETWORK

What to do: The list below includes many of the reasons we seek companionship; the blank spaces are for you to add others. There are two main columns, covering your present personal circumstances and your situation after the transition you are facing. Complete each column, using names or initials, leaving spaces where the question is irrelevant. You may find that some names disappear, and others appear more times in a different column in future.

	In my job, at home or elsewhere	
WHEN I WANT:	**WHO IS THERE NOW?**	**WHO WILL BE THERE AFTER THE CHANGE?**
To discuss this book		
To have a casual chat		
A companion for lunch, or a drink		
Information e.g. about a project I have in mind		
To be given advice		
To be comforted		
To moan!		
To argue!		
To laugh, share humour		
To share happiness		
To share sadness		
To be taken care of		
To go on holiday		
To share an activity		
To share bad news		
Someone to take care of		
Intimacy – physical closeness		
Emotional closeness		
To feel understood even when I'm horrible		
To be challenged		
Someone to be quiet with		
To be part of a family		
To take part in an activity		
Other:		
A		
B		
C		

What To Do Next: Using the list, follow this flowchart

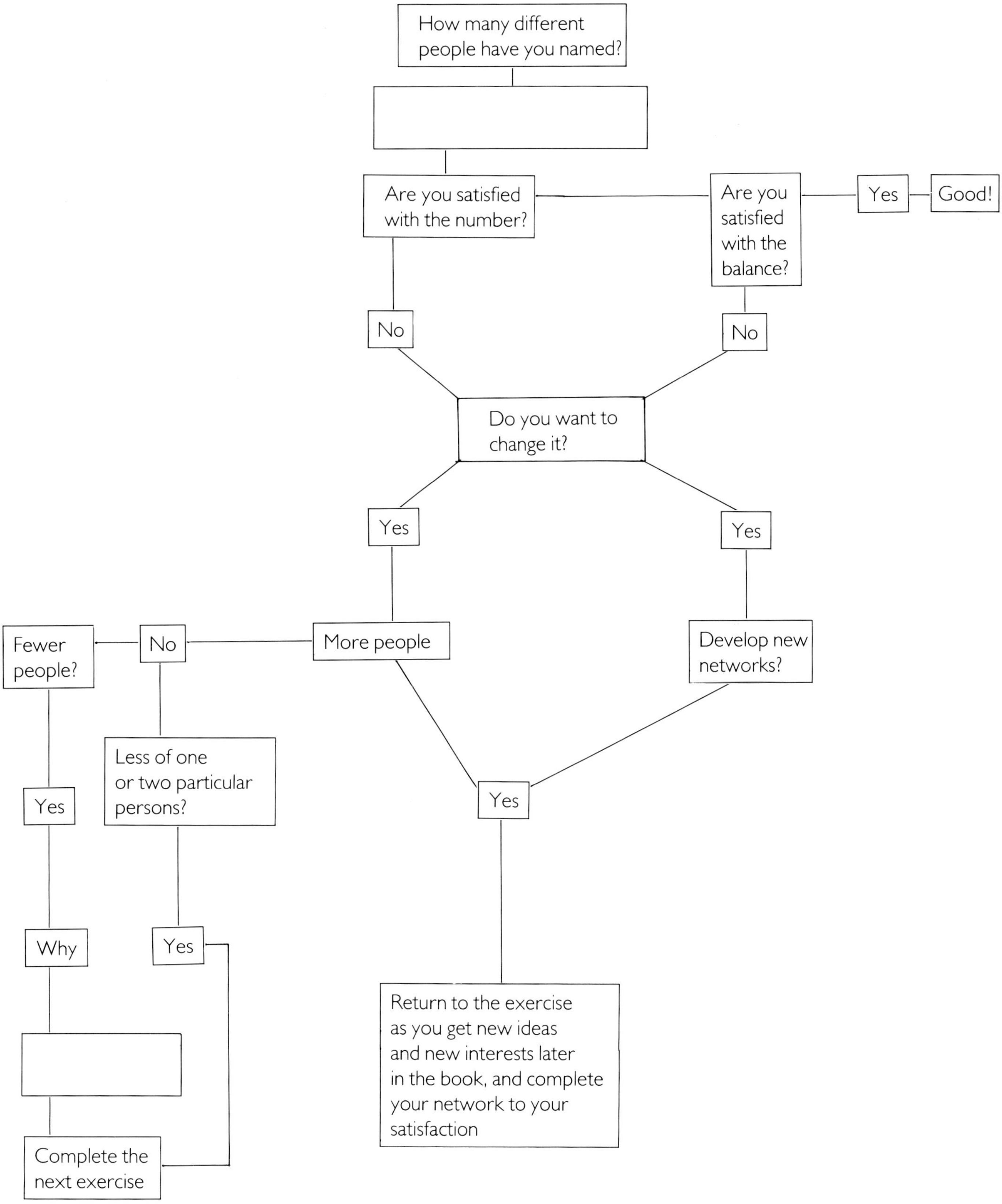

EXAMPLE

Kathy

I saw clearly how many of my friends are current workmates. Although I named several people in Column 1 there are blanks in Column 2, although I realise this is to be expected with a new venture, I was startled to discover I had circled 'Less of one person' – Martin and I don't share enough. We have some thinking to do.

Now that you have named the people who are part of your present network, you need to analyse exactly what roles they will play in future, and to reflect on your attitudes to any changes which are likely to take place. Following the next exercise there are sections which explain different aspects of mid-life roles and relationships.

EXERCISE 10

RETHINKING RELATIONSHIPS

This exercise asks questions about your relationships in general and focuses on specific people, and the proportion of time you will spend together in your new situation.

What to do: Read the questions and spend some time reflecting before you begin to write down your answers. Discuss your thoughts where possible, preferably with someone who will be part of any new network. Leave out any questions that don't seem relevant to your situation.

1 Who will you see more often, less often, the same?

....

how do you feel about this?..

....

2 How will you find any new companions you might need?

....

....

3 How will you retain relationships with people you want to continue to see?

....

....

4 Will your topics of conversation be:

the same as before; ....

less interesting ones; ....

more interesting ones; ....

how do you feel about this? ....

....

5 How much time will you spend at home:

the same/more/less ....

how do you feel about this? ....

6 How will you ensure privacy - for yourself or others?

....

....

....

7 If you do not have a partner, will you need new friends?

....

....

....

8 If you have children still at home, how do they feel about your decision?

....

....

....

9 Will you see more/less/the same of your near relatives?

....

....

....

10 Is there anyone who is likely to be dependent on you in the near future?

how will this affect any plans?

....

....

....

11 How do you feel about spending more/less time at home?

....

....

....

12 How do you feel about having someone at home more/less?

....

....

....

KATHY:

I've been uneasy about losing my friends at work ever since we started thinking of working together. Although I think we love each other, Martin and I have quite different interests. We're both fairly pushy people and I hope we don't internalise this in our new working relationship. We obviously need to identify the likely problem areas but we're both fairly explosive. There is one problem and that is the amount of time we will have available for sustaining old networks. It's not likely to be very much for the first two or three years.

MARTIN:

This exercise surprised me a fair bit. I'd been thinking only about the financial viability of working together. I now realise that most of my social contact came through work. Deep down I regard myself as a bit of a lad and I enjoyed the banter at work and in the pub afterwards. But I'll be leaving that all behind. Really Kathy and I have led parallel lives, each with our different networks. Now we will be working together we'll be far more dependent on each other. We'll have to think carefully about this.

INTERIM PROGRESS SUMMARY

You may find it helpful to complete this interim progress summary.

I am satisfied about my relationships with:

....

....

I am concerned about my relationships with:

....

....

I need to do something about my need for:

....

....

I intend to:

....

....

Aspects Of Relationships

Men and women – different lives?

There is often an assumption that women adjust more easily than men to transitions. Many people still assume that men are the main breadwinners and that women's role is most frequently to support and help men through transitions such as career moves, embarking on self-employment, retiring early, and so on. These assumptions don't accurately reflect reality. While it is true that there are more men than women in paid jobs, in 1981 women formed 40% of the workforce, 68% of married women worked outside the home. Women are likely soon to make up at least half the workforce as the youth population continues to fall. There are also many single, widowed and divorced women and men who face transitions without the support of a partner.

Women and men as carers?

There are certain aspects of mid-life which still affect women differently from men. They are seen by society as supporters of others – men, children, parents. Married women over 40 may only recently have returned to paid work and are anxious to keep their new independence. Men who grew up in the years when the male was automatically the 'breadwinner' and 'head of the house' able to give or withhold permission for a wife to take a job, may have difficulty in accepting her earnings, especially if the husband is not in employment. There is resentment from some women, not always easily expressed, that they are taken for granted as automatic providers of meals and companionship. While women may have gained a new independence and an outlet for their skills in their middle years, men who have found their jobs unrewarding and frustrating, may be exhausted by the need to compete. The middle years can bring opportunities for men and women (opportunities often inhibited in earlier years by the pressures to achieve or support or care for a family) to explore a different side of their nature, and to develop different roles for themselves within the family and in the work that they do. These changing values and activities can offer both sexes the opportunity to achieve personal fulfilment.

Single women (and some men)

Far more women than men have remained single in order to care for sick or elderly relatives, concentrating their energies in this area, rather than making outside relationships or developing their skills at work. Many of them retire early to continue as carers. Their lives may become very restricted and they risk losing the 'escape' they found through a job. If relatives die, the single carer faces loneliness, having had few opportunities to pursue other interests. If you recognise yourself in this description you will need to consider how you can extend your support network (see Chapter 10 for addresses of supportive organisations).

Changing roles

Married women, too, may find themselves once again offering family care, to elderly relatives or to grandchildren, which will restrict their choices and may affect plans for the future. It is likely that women's traditional roles will change, and that as society moves into the Information Era more attention will be paid to women as individuals. Younger men are slowly taking a more positive role in child-rearing, and younger women may decide not to have children at all, or to arrange child care, and return to their paid jobs. Meanwhile, women in their middle years still struggle with their own and other people's expectations. It is difficult to decide whether sex-roles are totally culturally imposed, or whether the need to nurture is biological and intuitive in women. Even if women do have an instinctive 'caring' response, there will be many advantages for both sexes as the 'supporter' role is offered more equally to both men and women. Men are sometimes unaware that support and comfort are needed, but rewarded by the response when they do reach out. There are naturally many exceptions to the picture of woman as supporter and many women enjoy the supportive role. Emphasising needs which seem to be specifically female may seem to overlook similar needs in men; but it may redress the usual balance of attention!

Married couples

> *My definition of marriage – it resembles a pair of shears, so joined that they cannot be separated, often moving in opposite directions, yet always pushing anyone who comes between them.*

Rev Sidney Smith.

Marriages today are often far less permanent than the inseparable shears, but couples who have reached middle age together will probably recognise the simile! For many couples mid-life is a time of renegotiation. Relationships often improve, but this is probably due more to tolerance and habit than to radical changes in behaviour! People who have embarked on a second marriage may still have a young family, needing financial support, and there may be heavy financial commitments. Both partners in any marriage may lead busy working lives, and the need to make decisions about radical change can create tensions, however stable the relationship has seemed. It is important to be aware of the possibility.

Difficult marriages exist – this is reality. Many marriages have survived only because the partners rarely meet. What is their future if circumstances change to bring them into more regular contact?

> *We've been together twenty years today, and there's a moral,*
> *Since we have no conversation,*
> *We have never had a quarrel,*
> *We hardly see each other,*
> *So we never have a fight,*
> *For 'Silence it is golden',*
> *And we've certainly proved that right.*

Pam Ayres

While one or both partners is fully employed, it is often possible to conceal strained relationships. Friendships at work may have substituted for lack of communication at home. A couple suddenly thrown together may feel as nervous as newly-weds, but with all the mysteries revealed and the excitement long vanished! Even those who enjoy the time and conversation they share may reflect that if they spend far more time together, their discussions may flag.

Divorce in middle age is unfortunately no longer an occasional phenomenon; 26% of second marriages are between people over 50. If changed circumstances cause unbearable strains, one or both partners may join the statistics of those who live alone.

If this sounds an unduly pessimistic outlook, it is realistic for many partnerships. Couples find discussions about significant life changes can offer an opportunity to discover more about each other's goals and needs, and perhaps to consider a remodelling of roles. These conflicts may not previously have been consciously expressed, and talking about them may surprise both partners.

Children and Grandchildren

People in their middle years may well have children who are still at school or are full-time students. An increase in second marriages may mean supporting more than one family, with the consequent financial implications, particularly for parents who are contributing towards student grants. There are other factors to consider: how will school-age children react to a change that may well mean moving school? How will they react to a mother who is no longer always at home?

Older offspring may be unemployed and around the house during the day. The 'jobless' label can become infectious and the self-esteem of whole families can be dealt a blow. It is difficult to visualise positive solutions and to move from the danger to the opportunities of the crisis.

You may be facing a transition because all your children have now left home, or you may find that other changes bring more opportunity to visit grown up children living elsewhere. If you are planning to spend time with them, it is advisable to share your plans – they may find too many visits from parents disconcerting! There is also the possibility that they have already given you the role of unpaid carpenter or babysitter. Remain a welcome rather than a dreaded visitor. Beware the 'You must have plenty of spare time now' approach.

Elderly relatives

It must now be very obvious that planning any major change in your life is rather like planning a wedding, so many people are involved! If you have elderly parents, they will perhaps be reaching a time when they find it less easy to cope alone and will need outside help, yours or others'. The vast majority of over-75's live in their own homes, or those of their children. Who will look after your parents or relatives? If you want to move house, or travel abroad for a while, will you feel able to go?

As public expenditure is cut, services to the most needy in the community devolve more and more on families, or on voluntary help. Even if you would like residential accommodation for a parent it is not easily available, or may be very expensive. Hospitals too, send patients back home whenever possible. There are many advantages to home care, but it may mean more personal involvement than you had planned.

If hospital or residential accommodation is available, the whole family may feel considerable guilt and distress. It is one thing to be told 'Put me in a home if I become helpless', quite another to do so when the time comes. If you decide to take relatives into your own home, discuss all the aspects thoroughly with everyone concerned (including the DSS, as you may be entitled to financial assistance). Delicate negotiations will be needed if the arrangement is to succeed. When elderly relatives die, compassion and a sense of duty may lead to hasty action, which is later regretted. An invitation to a bereaved father or mother to 'stay with us as long as you like' may become an unbearable situation, which neither party can resolve without guilt.

Living alone

I praise the Frenchman, his remark was shrewd –
How sweet, how passing sweet, is solitude!
But grant me still a friend in my retreat
Whom I may whisper – solitude is sweet!

Cowper

People who have lived alone for some years, perhaps all their adult lives, may well adapt very easily to a life change such as early retirement. They have always been responsible for their own social lives and may indeed enjoy being solitary, living alone from choice. A full life includes an ability to take pleasure in one's own company and be self sufficient at times. For people not used to living alone, fear of loneliness may be an important part of transitions such as leaving a large organisation to become self-employed, or coming to terms with the last child leaving home.

Loneliness – shyness

Loneliness is feeling, rather than being, alone and disliking the feeling. People who become lonely because they live alone and have made their jobs the focal point of life will need to consider where their new focus will be in their middle years. There will be no-one else to respond to a casual invitation to join you for a drink, an evening class or a visit to the cinema after work, and the loss will be even more dramatic if there is no-one at home to fill the gap. If you have lived alone because a partner has left, or has died, and have not chosen to live this way, you may feel lonely, especially if the gap in your life happened recently. It is distressing to meet people whose plans have been dramatically changed by the sudden death of a partner. Their doubts are highlighted by the need to face, perhaps for the first time, the reality of their isolation. Fortunately this is relatively rare, but it is a painful reminder that loneliness is more difficult to resolve when the essential companion goes.

EXAMPLE

Steven

I have accepted the offer to retire early since my heart attack, but I haven't dared think about the future. People have being talking about having more time to be together. The only person I have to talk to at home since Pamela died last year is the cleaning lady. I get very low and depressed. Someone suggested I should ring my local branch of CRUSE but I don't know if I can be bothered.

If Steven doesn't 'bother', he may become even more depressed. It's very easy to offer advice to join clubs – it sounds like an agony aunt in a teenage magazine telling shy young people to go to discos. If shy or lonely people could face a disco, or its equivalent, they would not be writing to the agony aunt. Unfortunately, the only way to meet people is to make what may seem an impossible effort, and *go where there are people to meet!* Try a new activity, or offer your services to help out a local organisation. Shyness and loneliness are much more common than we suppose, and having a useful role can act as an introduction without drawing attention to one's situation. If possible, find a friend to go with you at least for the first time, until you find the confidence and courage to go by yourself. Tell the organisers, or secretary, that you know no-one else there and you will probably be quickly introduced to others. If you cannot bring yourself to speak first, a smile helps! It may also help a little to be aware, and to *believe,* that other people, too, feel nervous. Loneliness lowers our self-esteem, especially if it reflects a recent loss. It is easy to decide, if we are unhappy about ourselves, that no-one would want to know us. Ease gently into new activities, take up new interests, and you will be someone who is well worth knowing and has much to contribute. An introduction agency, 'Old Friends', addresses this problem. The founders believe that many older people, especially women who have lost partners, may find themselves with few friends of either sex to share interests and activities.

There is no suggestion that families should stop caring, but it *is* important to acknowledge the enormous strains which develop when too many demands and changes occur together. You can find out more about the signs and symptoms of stress in Chapter 8.

Friends and neighbours

> *Your friend is your needs answered . . . and in the sweetness of friendship let there be laughter and sharing of pleasures.*
>
> Khalil Gibran

Transitions such as moving house, starting a new occupation, going back to work and retiring, often mean the loss of former friendship networks. These networks underpin our well-being and need to be replaced to maintain our quality of life. Neighbours and new or revived friendships can form the basis of new networks. And just as a young mother makes new friends when neighbours peer in the pram, the pram acting as the initial point of contact, we also need points of contact to make new friends of our neighbours. These could be as informal as clipping the hedge or working on the car, or they could be more structured, like joining your local branch of a political party or horticultural society.

Colleagues

Any transitional change involving a change of workplace has implications for your existing social networks. If you live in a small community, your colleagues, or ex-colleagues, may also be your friends and neighbours. You will need simply to adjust the times you meet, and possibly the topics of conversation. More often, home and work are geographically separate. Colleagues are people with whom you share interests, goals and skills and perhaps outside interests which you can pursue direct from the workplace. Will you be able to relate in the same way when mutual interests vanish? How will you meet each other when there is no automatic meeting place, and will any formal meeting be the same as casual interaction every day at work? If you want the relationships to continue, you need to plan ahead. These statements may appear obvious, but it is surprisingly easy to forget how much the workplace supplies friendships. People who become self-employed and work alone are soon aware there is no longer anyone around with whom to share coffee, or lunch, to chat about current projects, or about the contents of the day's newspaper. It may be necessary to create new 'colleagues'. See Exercise 4 'What motivates me?'

Living with someone other than a spouse

There are many combinations of lifestyle other than married couples or living alone! If you have always lived with a close friend, the adjustments will be similar to those of a married couple. If you are considering, as a new venture, going to live with someone, a brother or sister, a friend or one of your children, do try to plan and discuss every possible aspect. People who have been invited to live, for example, with a daughter in Australia, usually express some doubts about totally uprooting themselves. If it is at all possible, try to experiment before making a final decision, perhaps letting your present home while you stay for some months in the new setting.

For younger people the contact organisations listed in the personal columns of magazines, local and national newspapers have multiplied in recent years. In larger towns and cities local community centres offer a wide range of activities which give a ready introduction to new groups of people.

It can be very self-affirming to discover new survival skills, including the ability to *choose* to be alone at times and enjoy it. This element of choice is extremely important. There is nothing wrong with refusing to go to a party, but it helps if you were invited in the first place!

Touch and intimacy – sexuality – pets – how important are they?

The things that stop you having sex with age are exactly the same as those which stop you riding a bicycle – bad health, thinking it looks silly, no bicycle.

Alex Comfort

Human beings need to touch and be touched. The most intense expression of affection is through sexual relationships. Sexual enjoyment gives lifelong pleasure and satisfaction, but the touch of a hand, or an arm around the shoulder is missed by someone who has lost a partner, almost as much as the intimate sexual relationship.

Young people – and some older ones – are firmly convinced that no-one over fifty makes love.

Alex Comfort

Sexual relationships may well improve after the menopause, when there is no longer any risk of pregnancy. Does this apply only to the married? Unmarried, divorced and widowed women and men are often rather tentative about the possibility of new sexual relationships beginning in middle age. It is important that people feel free to behave as they wish, as long as no-one is harmed or upset. Many older people would prefer 'weekend' to full-time relationships. If they are self-sufficient, they may prefer part-time partnerships, but feel embarrassed and guilty. Guilt is not simply a prerogative of the unmarried, many couples wonder if their sexual appetites should have waned now that childbirth is out of the question. The expression of physical affection makes an important contribution to general health, (although casual sex can have its own problems). This is not an invitation to promiscuity or to orgies – although everyone to their own tastes! – but a plea for freedom from guilt and acceptance of normal and natural needs. There is no wish to offend the sensibilities of those whose religious beliefs preclude unmarried sexual relationships, simply to reassure those who have been taught that sex is only for the young and nubile, that they are 'allowed' to form new relationships.

Pets – touch and affection

One cannot overestimate the importance of the part animals play in meeting the need for touch. There is evidence (Alan Pack, University of Philadelphia) that people who keep pets survive heart attacks, and that the act of stroking and fondling an animal lowers blood pressure. Animals need care and offer affection; dogs which need exercise will force you to go out. People will talk to you, or the dog, or stop to admire a cat on your windowsill.

You may now want to go back to Exercise 10, Rethinking Relationships, and reassess your answers to the questions. You should also have plenty of discussion material!

You know *who* you live with. The final part of this chapter will look at *where* you live, and assess the dilemmas of moving house.

Arguments for and against moving to another home

I can't now afford the mortgage and repairs, better move to a smaller house. It will save on housework.

Let's move NOW, get all the changes over at the same time.

We're going to buy the shop in the village where we always spend our holidays and sell our pottery from it.

Now we can move nearer the new job. It would save an hour's travelling time.

My daughter said I could go and live with them in Canada. I'm lonely without my wife . . . may as well go.

Our house is too big now, but where will the children stay if we buy a smaller one?

Moving house, along with divorce and bereavement are the top three most stressful events in most people's experience. If you are already undergoing stress because of some other major transitional life change it is perhaps unwise to compound the stress by moving house at the same time. With some life changes such as retirement there is often an impulse to uproot and begin everything again, especially if you have financial anxieties and want to release capital. You may decide to move to the country, to a smaller house, to a flat, to live with a son in Canada. The word 'impulse' was chosen deliberately, to emphasise yet again the need to plan. Surburban life may seem less exciting than a Spanish villa, but where do most of your friends live? That Cornish farmhouse two miles from the sea is wonderful in June, but have you ever visited Cornwall in a November gale? What would you *do* in November, how good are the bus services?

Moving house is one of the most stressful transitions. It is not idly called 'uprooting'. You have seen already that multiple changes may cause stress, and stamina is needed to deal with the inevitable disappointments and enormous workload of buying and selling houses. A sudden decision to move would certainly add to the disorientation of major change and while the frantic activity of moving may obscure the insecurity, it is possible that settling in new surroundings may be hampered by regret, depression or even illness.

Despite this apparent pessimism, there are many advantages in moving while still relatively young.

EXERCISE 11

WHERE SHALL I LIVE?

What To Do: Answer all the questions which are relevant to your situation, (this *may* be all of them!). If you have already made the decision, use it as a checklist to make sure you have thought of everything!

1 Do you intend to move house?

Why?

Where to?

2 What alternatives are there?

3 If you are moving because your present home is too expensive, do you know what financial help is available?

4 Have you consulted everyone who may be affected by the decision?

5 What kind of accommodation do you want?

House, flat, bungalow, town, country, garden, abroad, etc

6 How much will it cost to move?

To move back if you wish?

7 How much will it cost for your family and friends to visit you?

For you to visit them?

8 Will you see as much of them as before?

How will this affect you?

9 If you have school-age children, how will the move affect them?

- Study
- Friends
- Neighbourhood

10 When will you see your friends?

11 Where will you find new friends?

12 Do you enjoy entertaining? ....

13 Will you have the time to form new friends? ....

....

14 Do you know anyone in the new locality? ....

....

15 Do they welcome newcomers? ....

....

16 What kind of transport do you have? ....

17 What public transport will be available? ....

18 Where are the basic services? ....

Post Office, bank, DSS, shops, leisure facilities, adult education, schools, doctor; medical facilities etc. ....

....

19 Do you know what the *year-round* climate is? ....

20 Is your health affected by: wind, cold, damp, heat etc? ....

....

21 Will your heating costs change? ....

What kind of fuel is available? ....

22 What other expenses might you have – increased maintenance etc? ....

....

23 Will you be able to earn money? ....

....

24 Are there opportunities to pursue all your interests? ....

....

25 How accessible, and expensive, are they? ....

....

26 Do you know where to get information about the new locality – and what information is available? ....

....

27 Are you able to make an extended visit before you make a final decision?

....

....

28 Have you assessed your future space requirements carefully during the time you intend to stay in your new property?

- Will any of your dependents (e.g. children) be moving out? ....

....

....

....

- Will you have new dependents (e.g. ageing parents) coming to live with you?

....

....

....

What To Do Next: After you have read and discussed the information in the next two pages, you may want to do the exercise again! If you are satisfied with your decision, you may find some useful ideas and resources.

Thoughts about home

If your present home is too large, the mortgage too high, too expensive to heat, or likely to need extensive repairs soon, have you explored all the financial help which might be available? Find out from your local authority or from housing associations exactly what assistance may be available to help you stay where you are. For example, you may be able to get an interest-only mortgage for major repairs; the capital is repaid when the house is sold. Housing associations can often arrange grants or loans. If you are a tenant and would like a move, you can find out about tenants, exchange schemes from your Citizens' Advice Bureau or your local housing department. Is your garden the wrong size for you? You could get an allotment. If your garden is too large, often the use of it to someone who lives in a flat.

Reasons for moving

Is the environment unsuitable for the way you would like to live? Do you feel like a complete change to cheer you up, does a growing family require a new environment?

Trying it out

If you have thought of living abroad, perhaps you could spend time there before making your final decision. It is possible to rent villas in Spain and Portugal, and perhaps elsewhere, very cheaply in the winter. Think what it will be like when you are really old, and how difficult you might find it to move back if you wished. Again even with moves within Britain, regional price disparities may make it difficult to move back.

Companionship

Will your family and friends be able to see as much of you as both you and they wish? Dropping in for coffee or playing a round of golf together each week is different from spending a formal weekend together. You may even discover family and friends you never knew existed, if you move to an attractive part of the country. Do you want to become a free guest house, and can you afford to? If you are moving to find peace and quiet, and time to garden or to write, do you want to spend extra time visiting and entertaining? It could, of course, be fun!

Similarly, if you are moving house to be *nearer* the family, it is wise to think through all the implications. You may not relish becoming a permanent babysitter, or DIY assistant. They may not be as delighted as you thought to have offers of help, or close scrutiny of their lifestyle! (A visit from parents often means frantic tidying, and inhibited behaviour from the children!)

Change of surroundings

Most people want to move from the city to the country or the sea, but there are those who welcome the opportunity to live in London or another large city for the first time for theatres, concerts, free exhibitions and all that a large city offers.

Expenses

Whether you move to, or from, the country, remember that food costs more where there are no supermarkets; that petrol or bus fares may soar and that services may be axed. Will it cost more to eat out; to have the car serviced; to buy essential supplies?
Will there be subsidised adult education, transport, theatres or any of the interests you want to follow?

Facilities

How well do facilities in the new environment compare with those you now enjoy? How convenient are shops, Post Office, GP, DSS, schools or hospitals? How near are your leisure interests, are there opportunities to pursue them? Car journeys may take up more of your time than you wish, or public transport may be limited.

Public resources

There are other considerations. If you are planning to move to an area where older people are the majority of residents, local authority resources may be disproportionately stretched. Social services are facilitated from income provided through rates and taxes paid by wage-earners and industrial sites. If there are too few ratepayers there may be fewer facilities when you begin to need them.

Paid work

Will you be able to find work if you need it?
Are you planning to run a small business? If you want to run a village shop, a pub or a smallholding, check the views of the small farmer, the publican or the shopkeeper. Thousands of village shops close each year. There may be customers for only six months of the year; you will have no time to enjoy the sun or the scenery, only the winter drizzle!
If you enjoy company, think again about your fantasy of running a guest-house. Bed and breakfast is mostly just that . . . bed, a meal, then moving on. You may get more washing up than pleasant conversation. Before you move to a new way of working life, talk to the people who live there already, and contact agencies like Cosira, or the Small Firms Service.

Isolation

If you are certain you must move somewhere smaller, perhaps to a flat, do remember that blocks of flats can be very lonely, especially for older newcomers.

Where to look for information

You may find out many details about an area before you go.

General information:	Copies of local newspapers
	Local radio station
Transport; housing; finance:	Town Clerk
	Estate Agents
	Librarian
Leisure; education; voluntary work:	Local Education Authority
	Local Volunteer Bureau
	Women's Institute
	Rotary Club
Health:	Hospitals
	Family Practioners Committee
	Community Health Centres

PROGRESS SUMMARY

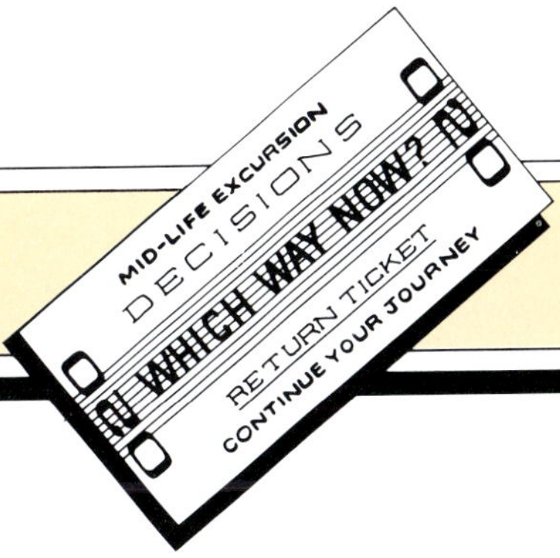

ANALYSIS AND REVIEW OF:

Personal Networks
Changing Relationships
Where to live – whether to move house

IMPORTANT INSIGHTS:

I WANT TO CHANGE:

I WANT TO CONTINUE:

I WANT TO BEGIN, OR TO DEVELOP:

NEW FACTS:

LINKS WITH OTHER PAGES:

WHAT'S NEXT? ON TO:
Finding out what kind of person I am – my interests, values and skills.

CHAPTER 6

WHAT AM I LIKE? WHAT DOES THIS MEAN TO ME?

WHO AM I?

WHAT HAS FORMED MY PERSONALITY?

WHAT DOES THIS MEAN TO ME?

In this chapter you will be exploring the impressions and influences which helped to shape your personality; your inner thoughts and feelings, your values, skills and interests. You have been constructing a scenario of the external events and people which will affect any decisions you make about future transitions and have learned how the life-changes you have experienced influence your present behaviour.

We shall not cease from exploration,
And the end of all our exploring
Will be to arrive where we started.
And know the place for the first time.

T. S. Eliot

In this chapter you will be exploring the impressions and influences which helped to shape your personality; your inner thoughts and feelings, your values, skills and interests. You have been constructing a scenario of the external events and people which will affect any decisions you make about future transitions and have learned how the life-changes you have experienced influence your present behaviour.

A significant life change will mark the beginning of a new phase in your life, and you will want to decide how to spend this next phase. Analysing past influences on your present personality will enable you to clarify both what you want and what might be the most fulfilling lifestyle.

Where have I come from?

You will perhaps know the story of the small boy who asked his Mum where he came from. She gave him an embarrassed and detailed biology lesson to which he listened and then said, 'Oh! Tommy says he comes from Glasgow, and I wondered where I came from.'

The exercises which follow will not ask for specific details of either your biological or geographical origins, although both will have played a major part in shaping the person you now are. There is sometimes a reluctance to explore the inner self. It may have something to do with an upbringing which taught that it was wrong to be 'self-centred', or to 'show off'. Yet if you have to go to a doctor, you are happy to provide details of your medical history, right back to childhood; when you apply for jobs, you emphasise your examination passes and other successes and give examples of all your experience. In order to discover the next steps you want to take in your life, it is essential to know what has helped you in the past . . . patterns of success, of enjoyment; ways of managing less happy events.

We are shaped by experiences within the family, at school and in society overall. Sad experiences leave some people with negative views of themselves and their activities, although a glimpse of their life history may offer a different, more positive, perspective. We all pick up negative messages. How often do you tell yourself 'I can't . . . sing . . . do maths . . . organise things . . . etc . . .' Are you sure? The first exercises ask you to explore your personality and history. These are followed by exercises which help you to analyse your interests, skills and values, and offer ways of managing time. Remember: discuss your responses with others – particularly those who are closely involved in your decision-making. Other people's feedback can help your self-analysis – and it's more fun!

EXERCISE 12

WHO AM I?

What To Do: Include facts, feelings and personal thoughts. You will find, as you write more sentences, that you begin to explore more intimate thoughts – you may even be surprised by what you write!

What To Look For: Signs of the person behind the everyday mask, your deeper needs and aspirations.

Write a list, beginning "I am a woman/man who . . ."
Write the sentence 12 times.

1 ....

2 ....

3 ....

4 ....

5 ....

6 ....

7 ....

8 ....

9 ....

10 ....

11 ....

12 ....

EXAMPLE

Andreas **Harriet**

An Architect

I am a man who:

1 *Designs office blocks*
2 *Plays tennis regularly*
3 *Likes meeting people*
4 *Enjoys his work*
5 *Likes to live well*
6 *Is divorced*
7 *Has no family*
8 *Dreads stopping work*
9 *Enjoys a challenge*
10 *Likes being successful*
11 *Drinks too much at times*
12 *Doesn't discuss feelings*

A Community Nurse

I am a woman who:

1 *Is always busy*
2 *Loves my patients*
3 *Is very happily married*
4 *Has three children*
5 *Will miss my work*
6 *Hates being bored*
7 *Hates housework*
8 *Loves music*
9 *Looks forward to being a grandmother next month*
10 *Dreads losing my husband*
11 *Hates being on my own*
12 *Prays to stay healthy*

What to do next: Looking through your list, answer the following questions:

1 Were you surprised by what you wrote?..

....

2 How do you feel about your list?..

....

3 Would you have written the same list ten years ago?..

....

4 How many people know *all* these things about you?..

....

5 Is the list likely to change over the next ten years?..

....

EXAMPLE

	Andreas	Harriet
1	*No – I am a workaholic!*	*I've never put into words before that I hate being alone.*
2	*Very slightly worried. It is not the right time to retire.*	*Sad and amused. I will miss my work, and I do love my family.*
3	*Not quite, I was still married, and rock climbing most weekends.*	*Not the grandmother!*
4	*My ex-wife.*	*Several, except the fear of loneliness. I don't want to worry people. I save that for God!*
5	*I may play less tennis, but I intend to have work of some kind.*	*In a practical sense I hope to find new interests besides my work – and family size will alter. Maybe I'll even be able to stay in the house alone!*

Think about your answers and discuss them where possible. You will need to compare this list with the liferoute to be drawn in the next exercise, as there will be links between the two which will deepen any insights.

EXERCISE 13

MY LIFEROUTE

This exercise may seem very similar to the transition lifeline, but there are many differences. The transitions lifeline was a straight line which marked the number of changes in your life. The liferoute is your personal view of the ups and downs and the plateaux in your life.

In interpreting the liferoute you will be looking for themes which appear as 'mountain peaks' or as 'deep troughs'. It will be important to compare the liferoute with your 'Who Am I?' list.

What to do: Draw a line which will indicate the route your life has taken – see the example below. Mark the ups and downs, and name them. You can begin the line at birth, or later if you wish, and it need not be to scale, or include *every* event, just those which come fairly rapidly into your mind. It should take about five minutes.

EXAMPLE

Gwen

A teacher aged 40: returning to work after 12 years spent at home with her children

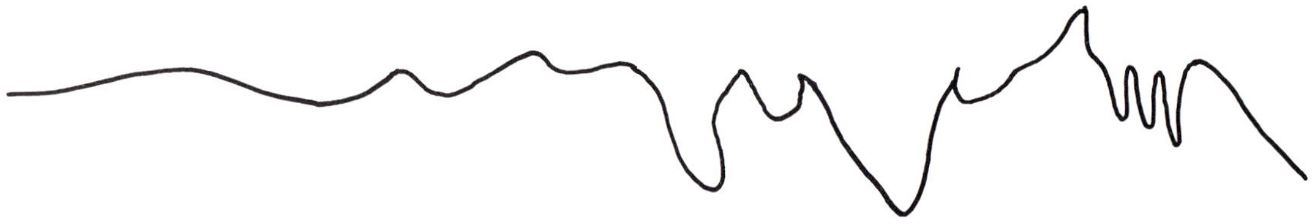

What to do next: Examine and reflect on the liferoute you have drawn and answer the following questions:

1 Are there any recognisable themes? The themes could include:
Success and failure.
Unavoidable events – like separation, hospital, etc.
People – their presence or absence; opinions; relationships.

What does this mean to you? ....

....

....

2 Can you see where your liferoute has influenced your present outlook? ....

....

....

3 What can you learn from the shape of your liferoute – is it smooth, full of ups and downs – any surprises? ....

....

....

4 Compare the liferoute with the 'Who Am I?' list. What connections can you make? (Andreas' liferoute reflected his work achievements; there were few references to relationships. Harriet's was about relationships and family.) ....

....

....

5 What is the most important learning from the two exercises? ....

....

....

6 Compare the liferoute with the transitions lifeline on Page 27.
Which of the events on your liferoute are also on your transitions lifeline? ....

....

Which transitions have been left out? ....

....

....

What conclusions do you draw? ....

....

....

7 Would someone who knew you well have drawn your liferoute differently? ....

....

....

Take as much time as you like for this section. Find someone to help you 'Mapread' if possible.

EXAMPLE

Gwen

1 *The themes are education, work, birth and death.*

I seem to be preoccupied with education and jobs, which I suppose is success – failure. I had no idea my husband's achievements were so important to me. His promotion looks more important than our wedding! I've drawn his redundancy 3 years ago as our lowest trough yet, even though he found another job fairly quickly. Reaching the decision to go back was also a trough, perhaps surprisingly. I felt terribly apprehensive about how teaching had changed since I left it. I used to be good teacher and I was afraid of going back and failing. I feel more confident now because I've been offered a senior position, but I'm still nervous!

2 *This reply follows on. I have always been influenced by success at work and keeping busy, that's why I was worried about John's redundancy. I suppose, too, his moods depend on how well he is doing and I know he doesn't like this job much, while I'm going back to something I love. I don't want to feel guilty about being the one 'at the top' now. I think I expect my children to do well too. I'm beginning to wonder if I reacted so strongly to the car crash (another low) because I found it so difficult to show my grief about the family deaths.*

3 *Everything I have said already. I was shocked to see that my son's expulsion was one of my lowest points. It makes me look rather heartless. I intend to be more positive and understanding with my husband.*

4 *In the 'Who am I?' list I found it difficult to find 12 items, partly because I didn't want to put things which make me sad – and I* did *say 'I am a person who likes to do well'.*

5 *I've talked to John and my younger son, and they agree that I've always set great store by success, which has made things difficult for them at times. I hope I've learned to relax my demands, and to see that* people *are important for themselves.*

6 *I see that I put all the moves, deaths and the car crash on the transitions line, but not Andrew's expulsion from school or my husband's redundancy. I didn't see them as* my *transitions, I suppose.*

7 *My husband would have left out his redundancy. He had no idea it mattered to me! He would also have made the bereavements lower and less abrupt. He said I had left out time I spent nursing my mother and sister and that I undervalue my support for others. He was surprised that I felt such conflicting feelings about going back to teaching – he hadn't realised how much staying at home had affected my confidence in the outside world!*

EXAMPLE

Lynn

Local government officer moving to a smaller organisation in the private sector.

Lynn discovered that the themes of her 'peaks' were events she organised, and taking care of people. She had worked for twenty years for a local authority, where she found little opportunity to develop these interests. She made notes which helped her to remember these themes. When she added the information and self-knowledge she gained from other exercises, it helped her in her decision to accept an opportunity to manage a small Conference Centre.

Who am I? – Filling in the details

Activities – interests – values – skills

The next exercise will enable you to analyse specific activities which interest you, your major values, and your skills. You can then decide what to go on doing, what to drop, and what new skills and interests you might want to develop.

Could you retrain to pursue a new career? Or learn to speak Chinese?

Will you be delighted if you never see your neighbours again, or never need to have your decisions approved by your departmental head, or never have to organise a meeting?

If you will be sorry to lose your neighbours to consult about your decisions, or arrange meetings, how can you find ways of continuing these activities?

EXERCISE 14

ACTIVITIES AND INTERESTS – DECIDING PRIORITIES

The next three pages include a comprehensive list of activities which occupy people's lives at work, at home and at play. There are spaces for you to add any of your interests which have been omitted.

What To Do: There are three major columns –

1 PRESENT PATTERN: 2 FUTURE PATTERN: 3 PREFERRED PATTERN.
Each column is subdivided into five: Daily: Weekly: Regularly or Often: Occasionally: Rarely or Never.

1. Go through the list and mark, in the PRESENT PATTERN column, the subdivision which represents the frequency with which you carry out each activity *now*.
2. Then go through the list again, and complete the FUTURE PATTERN column, which represents the *likely* level after the transition you are facing.
3. Mark in column 3, PREFERRED PATTERN, the frequency with which you would *like* to pursue each activity. When you compare columns 2 and 3 you will be able to see how far your 'future' activities match your actual

EXAMPLE

Patrick

	PRESENT	**FUTURE**	**PREFERRED**
Arrange Meetings	*Weekly*	*Rarely*	*Regularly*
Art – practise	*Occasionally*	*Daily/Weekly*	*Daily/Weekly (paint)*
Budget for self	*Regularly*	*Regularly*	*Regularly*
Meet new people	*Daily*	*Rarely*	*Regularly*

ACTIVITY/INTEREST	PRESENT PATTERN					FUTURE PATTERN					PREFERRED PATTERN				
	Daily	Weekly	Regu-larly or often	Occa-sionally	Rarely or Never	Daily	Weekly	Regu-larly or often	Occa-sionally	Rarely or Never	Daily	Weekly	Regu-larly or often	Occa-sionally	Rarely or Never
Arrange group meetings															
Arrange meetings															
Arrest people															
Attend meetings															
Browse – sales, auctions, shops															
Budget – for self/family															
Buy for organisations															
Buy for self/family															
Buy to sell again															
Chair meetings															
Clean buildings, streets															
Clean rooms, clothes, objects															
Climb mountains															
Collect cash – checkouts, banks															
Collect objects															
Cook for restaurant, residents															
Cook for self/family															
Crafts – pottery, wood, sew, etc.															
Dance															
Deliver – milk, letters, goods															
Design – events, programmes, etc.															
Design – furniture, buildings, dress															
D.I.Y.															
Draw – pictures, cartoons															
Draw – plans, layouts															
Drive – car, bicycle, van															
Drive large vehicles – bus, train, lorry, plane															
Drive long distances															
Direct – people, traffic															
Direct – theatre, films															
Drink – pubs, clubs, wine bars															
Eat – canteens, restaurants, home															
Entertain – family/friends															
Entertain – formal, business															
Evaluate – performance, progress															

ACTIVITY/INTEREST	PRESENT PATTERN					FUTURE PATTERN					PREFERRED PATTERN				
	Daily	Weekly	Regularly or often	Occasionally	Rarely or Never	Daily	Weekly	Regularly or often	Occasionally	Rarely or Never	Daily	Weekly	Regularly or often	Occasionally	Rarely or Never
Farm															
File documents															
Fish															
Garden – for profit															
Garden for self/family															
Gamble – cards, bingo, horses															
Go camping															
Go on holiday															
Indoor games of skill															
Interview people															
Invent															
Initiate – ideas, policies															
Listen to people's problems															
Listen to radio, records, tapes															
Meet new people															
Music, art – look, listen, practise															
Perform for fun, sing, paint, etc.															
Perform in public															
Photography															
Play games or take exercise alone or with one other – golf, swim, run															
Play or watch team games															
Politics															
Pressure groups															
Read – documents, reports, letters															
Read – newspapers, books, magazines															
Repair/maintain machinery, buildings															
Repair/restore objects															
Relaxation, meditation															
Religious and spiritual interests															
Raise capital for business purposes															
Raise funds															
Sit and think – or just sit!															
Sell in a shop/market															
Sell to an organisation, shop															

ACTIVITY/INTEREST	PRESENT PATTERN					FUTURE PATTERN					PREFERRED PATTERN				
	Daily	Weekly	Regu-larly or often	Occa-sionally	Rarely or Never	Daily	Weekly	Regu-larly or often	Occa-sionally	Rarely or Never	Daily	Weekly	Regu-larly or often	Occa-sionally	Rarely or Never
Solve problems, crimes															
Speak foreign languages															
Speak to large groups															
Speak in small groups															
Speak with one other															
Study birds, animal life															
Study at home															
Supervise – machines, equipment															
Supervise – people, activities															
Take active holidays – sail, ramble, etc.															
Take care of adolescents															
Take care of babies															
Take care of old people															
Take care of people's feet, hair, teeth															
Take care of people's health															
Teach an individual															
Teach in a class															
Teach, train other than in classes															
Use public transport															
Use rush hour transport															
Use public library															
Use telephone															
Visit doctor, dentist, hospital															
Visit family, friends															
Visit patients, prisoners, housebound people															
Visit museums, galleries, zoos, etc.															
Walk long distances															
Walk up to two miles															
Watch TV															
Winemaking															
Work with computers, technology															
Work with typewriter															
Write – instructions, reports															
Write – stories, books, poetry, scripts															
Yoga															

Looking at the items you have marked

Make a list of:

- Those activities which you will do MORE often than you wish:

  e.g. FUTURE; Daily. PREFERRED; Rarely.

  ....

  ....

1 Would you like to do this less often because it is tedious but necessary, or is there a stronger reason?

  ....

  ....

2 Could you do anything to change the situation?

  ....

  ....

3 How will the activity affect your other plans?

  ....

  ....

- Make a list of those activities you will do LESS often than you wish.

  ....

  ....

1 Do you have any control over the amount of time you spend on this activity?

  ....

  ....

2 What is likely to stop you following this interest as often as you like?

  ....

  ....

3 Where might you find new ways to follow an activity you enjoy? (If you like arranging meetings, and will be able to do so only rarely, where might you find more meetings to arrange – perhaps join a committee or a voluntary organisation?)

  ....

  ....

4 Is there any underlying theme to your PREFERRED PATTERN of activities?

  ....

  ....

As you highlight particular activities, you will discover not only what you like about your present lifestyle, but also the frustrating parts of your job. You may be planning to spend more time developing a new skill, or having fun. You may reinforce the relief you anticipate when some of your current activities can stop.

What to do next: you have probably realised that this exercise is linked to Exercise 4 which helps you decide which elements of your working life you want to retain. You may find it useful to take another look at that exercise, to reinforce your analysis of the relative importance of the activities and interests in your life.

Using the sheet you have just completed, and taking coloured pens if possible, to make the 'matching' more easily recognisable, follow the instructions below. The information will give you a base to begin setting objectives for your future.

Look at interests you wish:

to continue as before;
to expand;
to begin;
to cut down or stop;

and see where you will need to plan changes.

1 Underline all the activities which are in the same sub-column (daily, etc) of all the main columns 'PRESENT', 'FUTURE', 'PREFERRED'.
These items you will continue with the same regularity and are satisfied to do so.

2 With a different colour, go through the 'FUTURE' and 'PREFERRED' main columns, and underline those items which appear in the same sub-column each time.
These activities you will be able to follow as frequently as you wish; you plan to expand or begin, or to cut down on them.

3 Now circle, with a third colour if possible, those items which you have placed in different sub-columns of 'FUTURE' and 'PREFERRED'.
These are items which need further analysis. They match either the 'Factors I need to replace' (Exercise 4) or are activities you are forced to continue more than you wish.

EXAMPLE

Sue

Librarian changing from full-time to part-time work to care for her dependent mother.

The interests I can more easily pursue than I do now are an extension of my present life – going to classes; music; swimming; yoga. I shall join the Open University.
I intend to make another attempt to play the clarinet, and looking through this list I discovered some new interests I might develop. Collecting junk is one of them!

I shall be glad to lose the travel, filing (this includes returned books), phones, and some of the report-writing, on the two days I'll not be working.

I would prefer not to care for elderly people so much, but my mother cannot be left unattended. I can do a little to change the situation, by joining the Association of Carers, but I enjoy looking after her most of the time.

I realise I will miss meeting the public and solving problems – I am going to offer to help at the local Advice Centre.

Not sure yet how I can get more staff to manage!

(I put FUTURE: Occasionally, PREFERRED: Regularly!)

Setting objectives

You will need to return to this list, and may wish to make further changes when you have analysed your values and your skills, and explored your past dreams.
In Chapter 7: What are my practical options? you will find advice and ideas for work, leisure and learning, to help you plan how to spend your future.

Defining priorities – what are my values?

You now know more about the interests you want to pursue. To help you decide which of them are most important to you, the next exercise will help you analyse your values. These include your basic beliefs, the principles by which you live, or would like to live. You may attain them only on holiday because of the demands of your job, or the need to live in a large city. When you examine your spiritual values and your total philosophy, in Chapter 9, and explore what you would like to have achieved in your life, you may like to come back to this section, as your values are inseparable from your philosophy.

How do I discover my values? Why will it help me to do so?

Ask yourself:

What is important to me about – people – places – objects – words – human qualities?

You are planning to use your transition to develop a fulfilling lifestyle. You are more likely to feel satisfied and fulfilled if you engage in activities which reflect your major values.

In the next exercise you can analyse the importance to you of the values listed.

EXERCISE 15

VALUES – MY PRIORITIES*

What to do: This exercise is similar to Exercise 14: Interests and Activities. For each of the 'Values' on the list, ask yourself whether it is ESSENTIAL; VERY IMPORTANT; FAIRLY IMPORTANT; of LOW IMPORTANCE or UNIMPORTANT. Complete the columns on this sheet, then answer the questions which follow.

	ESSENTIAL	VERY IMPORT-ANT	FAIRLY IMPORT-ANT	LOW IMPORT-ANCE	UNIMPORT-ANT
VALUES LIST Active, energetic lifestyle					
Artistic activity – paint, act, etc.					
Beauty: aesthetic, arts, man-made					
Beauty: natural, sea, countryside					
Challenge					
Close companionship, friendships					
Communicating in speech					
Communicating by writing					
Contact with others: group, work, leisure					
Contentment, relaxation					
Creativity, thinking of new ideas					
Decision-making, for self and others					
Equality, justice					
Excitement, risk					
Expertise, doing things really well					
Family security, nurturing					
Financial security					
Humour					
Independence					
Learning: skills, intellect					
Loyalty: to organisations, ideal, person					
Peace: world, tranquillity					
Physical skill, challenge					
Precision, attention to detail					
Pleasure, easy life, leisure					
Power, influence, prestige					
Recognition, admiration, respect					

*Adapted from Barrie Hopson and Mike Scally, *Build Your Own Rainbow*.

	ESSENTIAL	VERY IMPORT-ANT	FAIRLY IMPORT-ANT	LOW IMPORT-ANCE	UNIMPORT-ANT
VALUES LIST Responsibility, leadership, supervising					
Routine, stability					
Self-respect					
Sexual intimacy					
Spiritual interests					
Teaching, guiding the young					
Teaching anyone					
Time freedom					
Usefulness to others, to society					
Worthwhile activity, accomplishment					
Wisdom, maturity					

What to do next: List your five major values, then answer the questions.

1 ....

2 ....

3 ....

4 ....

5 ....

1 How far does your present lifestyle reflect these values?

....

....

2 If this is not possible, what is preventing it?
(For example: natural beauty – sea – only possible at weekends.)

....

....

3 How far do your 'Interests' reflect these major values?

....

....

4 Do you want to make any changes to the list?

....

....

5 Look at your Transitions Lifeline, Exercise 5 and your Liferoute, Exercise 13. What part has the past played in forming your values?

(Constant moves in childhood may make you value family security).

....

....

6 Others in your life: How far do your values reflect those of the people who are most likely to be part of your life in future?

....

....

7 Will you need to change your present lifestyle to match your values?

....

....

In order to fulfil those qualities I value, I may need to ....

What skills do I have? Where can I use them? Could I learn new ones?

You may wonder why you need to assess your skills; especially if your plans do not include a paid job. You may even have difficulty in identifying skills other than those used in the practical aspects of your job. As has already been demonstrated in Chapter 2, research shows that lack of opportunity to use skills, together with loss of companionship can be more important than finances to people who face a significant change in their life situation. Whether you are considering voluntary work in the community or ways to use your leisure satisfactorily, an analysis of those skills you have, those you might like to acquire and those you can now relinquish with relief is an important part of your investment in planning your new lifestyle. When people are asked to identify their skills, they most readily reply in terms of their job, or a specific task.

A car mechanic might respond: good with engines, especially tuning them.
A dressmaker: cutting patterns, hand finishing.
A clerical worker: filing, answering telephone requests, adding figures.

These are the skills they have learned in order to complete a practical task: job content skills. They have learned through education, through special training or simply by long experience. The car mechanic, the dressmaker and the clerical worker all have other skills they take for granted, do not define as skills, or might feel diffident about; like listening to customer's problems; being reliable, honest and punctual; identifying and solving problems.

One difference between job content skills, like tuning engines, and the more abstract skills, like listening and problem-solving, is that the content skills can be seen and measured. They are used for specific tasks. Skills like listening can be transferred from one kind of task to another. A mother who cooks for her family (content) may also have catering, managing budgeting and planning skills (transferable to tasks other than cooking). She could open and run her own restaurant using all her transferable skills, but doing no cooking!

Administrative or marketing skills can be transferred to different products or services. If you wish to use your job content skills in the future you may be able to find work, paid or unpaid, in your present field. Practical skills which you may have used only for your personal needs and interests could become money-earners if there is a market for them. Transferable skills (which may not even be recognised as skills), make it possible to pursue new areas. It is always possible to acquire new skills, even if there are reasons you could not perfect them. You may be too late to be an opera singer, but you can still improve your singing voice and become a choral singer or local soloist.

There are many ways to catalogue skills; for the purpose of the next exercise they have been grouped in four sections – DATA, PEOPLE, THINGS and IDEAS.

EXERCISE 16

WHAT ARE MY SKILLS WHICH ONES ARE IMPORTANT TO ME?

What To Do: Go through the list and tick the appropriate column(s) beside each item.
Consider *all* the areas of your life – Paid work
Work at home
Leisure
Community
General interests
Past interests

You may have a skill which is poor, but you would like to improve it – so you would tick two columns. The column marked 'Irrelevant' covers skills which you neither have nor want. Some areas where you are very competent may be irrelevant in future, but if you want to build an accurate picture of yourself, you will need to tick the 'Highly Skilled' column. (You may, of course, want to tick 'irrelevant' as well!)

	Highly Skilled	Very Competent	Adequate	Poor	Would Like to Improve or Learn	Irrelevant
DATA Analysing, dissecting information						
Calculating, computing						
Diagnosing – looking for problems						
Examining, observing, surveying – an eye for detail						
Following instructions diagrams, etc						
Managing money – small or vast sums						
Manipulating numbers rapidly – mental sums						
Memorising; numbers and facts						
Organising, classifying						
Problem solving						
Reading – to extract facts						
Report-writing						
Research – gathering information						
Reviewing, evaluating						
Taking an inventory						
Other areas in this group:						
PEOPLE Conveying warmth and caring						
Drawing out people						
Giving credit to others						
Helping others						
Initiating relationships						
Leading, directing others						
Listening						
Motivating people						
Organising people						
Performing – in a group or on stage						
Promoting change						
Selling, persuading, negotiating						
Showing sensitivity to others' feelings						
Teaching, training						
Other areas in this group:						

	Highly Skilled	Very Competent	Adequate	Poor	Would Like to Improve or Learn	Irrelevant
THINGS Assembling things						
Building, constructing						
Driving – car, plane, motorcycle, etc.						
Finding out how things work						
Fixing, repairing things						
Growing things						
Hand-eye co-ordination						
Handling things with precision, speed						
Keeping physically fit						
Manual dexterity						
Muscular co-ordination						
Physically strong						
Quick physical reactions						
Tending animals						
Using hand tools						
Using machine, lathe, power tools						
Using technology – typewriter etc.						
Other areas in this group:						
IDEAS Composing music						
Conveying feelings or thoughts – through body, face or voice						
Conveying feelings or thoughts – through drawing, painting, etc.						
Designing – things, events, materials						
Developing others' ideas						
Fashioning things or materials						
Having insight, using intuition						
Improvising, adapting						
Innovating – creating alternatives						
Reading for ideas						
Sizing up situations/people quickly						
Working creatively – colours, shapes						
Writing creatively						
Other areas in this group:						

What To Do Next: Have you been too modest? Ask as many people as possible to help you complete this exercise.

Analysing Your Priorities (Try using different coloured pens)

1 Draw a circle round the skills you *enjoy* using. If they are not in the 'Highly Skilled' column, would you like to improve them? If so, put a tick in that column.
2 Put a cross through those you do *not enjoy* using, even though you may be highly competent. You may want to make them 'Irrelevant'. If you must continue to use those particular skills, could you find ways to make them more satisfying? Or could someone else help you out? Underline those areas where you would like to develop new abilities.

Answer the following questions:

1 Are your skills concentrated in a particular section, **DATA, PEOPLE, THINGS,** or **IDEAS,** or do you cover a wider field?

....

....

2 Have you discovered skills you would like to use in ways you have not previously considered?

....

....

3 Would you like to learn new skills? Exercise 19, Rediscovering Learning

....

....

4 Refer to your Interests and Activities list on the previous pages.

- Which skills could you transfer to a new activity you would like to develop?

....

....

- Would learning new skills enable you to continue activities you may lose?

....

....

- Are your present skills consistent with your major values?

....

....

Now it would be helpful to list:

Skills I enjoy using and where I am highly competent:

....

....

....

....

Skills I enjoy using and would like to improve:

....

....

....

....

Skills I could transfer to new activities:

....

....

....

....

Skills I would like to develop:

....

....

....

....

Alternative analysis – "motivated skills"

What To Do: This way of working takes longer than ticking words in columns, and is most usefully done with the help of a partner.
Write down up to ten major achievements in your life, in narrative form. An achievement is something you were proud of, were satisfied with and enjoyed. It does not have to be an achievement in society's eyes nor a recent one. Then underline all the *active* words and phrases in one of them.

Make a list of the words, then underline the active words in the other nine achievements.
Make a note of the number of times the same word appears. After you have completed the ten items, make a further list, of words which are alike (there will probably be about 8-10 with similar meanings). Find a common word for each set of phrases. These are your 'Motivated Skills'.

EXAMPLE

Paul

European marketing manager, textiles. Retiring early with reluctance, on health grounds.

Paul was surprised to find a recognisable pattern to the 'achievements' he remembered. Here is one of the earlier ones.

One of my most exciting memories was swimming three miles for charity just after the war, when I was 17. I had always had asthma, and couldn't play games, so when I learned to swim I was determined to be good at it. Most people only swam a mile or so, but I practised every day and got all my relations and friends to sponsor me. I persuaded them all to give double if I managed three miles. There seemed to be hundreds of people watching, and I got very tired but I knew I had to finish. It wasn't just to prove I could do it, but I wanted to help the polio victims we were collecting for and I really loved swimming.

Paul extracted from these and similar phrases words which appeared in all ten lists, which were:

1. Keeping physically fit (he wasn't too sure about this!)
2. Muscular co-ordination.
3. Sensitivity to others' needs.
4. Innovating (in the example above, asking people to double the money if he swam three miles!)
5. Problem solving.
6. Determination; responding to challenges.
7. Persuading.
8. Helping others.
9. Organising; motivating people.
10. Completing projects.

I hadn't thought that 'helping others' or 'being sensitive' was a skill. Several colleagues insisted that I included them. Sensitivity is not always something a manager likes to admit! When I was younger it would have sounded a bit 'soft'. I must make sure I take on a few more challenges. Maybe I'll try for a five mile swim next year!

Paul's stamina and will to succeed, and to overcome obstacles, had led him to a senior management role. Unfortunately his health problems had re-emerged and he was forced to retire early on medical grounds. He used his interest in swimming to encourage local unemployed young people to develop their confidence by swimming well. He also organised fund raising for charity.

If you choose this method of discovering your skills, you can then return to the questions which follow Exercise 16. It is important to understand any apparent conflicts. For example – how could Paul's physical skills match his ill-health? Any discoveries in this exercise may help you to understand why you have perhaps become dissatisfied with your job.

Are you unable to use the skills at which you are most competent? Does frustration with your present work lead to the suppression of some of your values? You will also be able to see more clearly where your wishes may clash with someone else's plans or values. If so, how can you find ways to negotiate, so that no-one feels upset?

This chapter includes many very important details. As it is so complex, here is an:

INTERIM PROGRESS SUMMARY

ANALYSIS AND REVIEW OF:

My liferoute – how I became who I am.
My interests, values and skills.

IMPORTANT INSIGHTS:

I WANT TO CHANGE:

I WANT TO CONTINUE:

I WANT TO BEGIN, OR TO DEVELOP:

NEW FACTS:

LINKS WITH OTHER SECTIONS:

WHAT'S NEXT? ON TO:

Managing Time – Diaries and Clocks – My Time Balance Sheet.
Overall Progress Summary.

Check on progress so far

If you have worked systematically through the exercises, you will have reflected on your reactions to life changes affecting your hopes and your anxieties.
You will know how you react to major changes, and the skills you see for coping with those changes. You will have built a picture of the influences on your present attitudes, and will know more about who you are, what you want to do, who you will be spending your time with. You can perhaps see more clearly how many adjustments will be needed and by whom.
You know about your financial priorities, and will now want to start planning your time, so that you can achieve your personal optimum balance of essential and leisure activities.

How well do I manage my life?
How can you plan without mortgaging every minute?
Managing your time

And indeed there will be time
To wonder, 'Do I Dare?' and 'Do I Dare?'
Time to turn back and descend the stair,
With a bald spot in the middle of my hair –
They will say 'How his hair is growing thin!'

T S Eliot

I'll start tomorrow.
I've no energy. Stop
fussing. I like TV.
Weary Willie.

Haven't time to do
half the things I want
to do. I'm exhausted.
Busy Lizzie.

Managing your time means knowing:

- how to spend your time;
- how you want to spend it;
- what helps you to get maximum satisfaction from your day;
- what prevents you from doing the things you want to do.

(This could include planning time to do NOTHING!)
Many of you will be familiar with statements like, 'When I've finished this I'll take a break, if there's time' (. . . and there never seems to be time for the break!!).

The next exercise will take at least a week!

This exercise entails keeping a very detailed diary. It assumes that you have not yet changed your circumstances. If you have, then you may like to compare your present diary with how you formerly spent your time. It may involve more work than you think necessary, but if you do keep up the entries, you will clarify not only WHAT you were doing, but:

- how much of your time is within your own control;

  ....

- how much time you spend doing things you MUST do but don't enjoy;

  ....

- how many of the things you enjoy doing are things you choose to do?

  ....

Where there might be gaps after your transition:

- what is likely to be different about the way you spend your time;

  ....

- how will you feel about this;

  ....

- which of the differences do you anticipate with pleasure?

  ....

EXERCISE 17

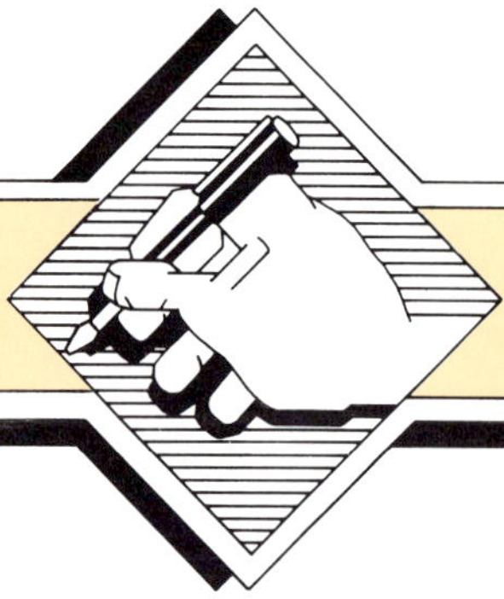

DIARIES AND CLOCKS

What To Do: Keep a diary for the next week, dividing each day into two hour periods and noting what you do with each hour.

At the end of each day, using a different colour for each item, underline:

1 Things you *enjoyed* doing.
2 Things you *chose* to do.
3 Things you *had* to do.
4 Things you *disliked* doing.

Henry and Mary are married. They have decided that Henry will give up his full-time job as a headteacher to become a part-time educational advisor. To maintain their income Mary will also return to work as a paid part-time administrator for a voluntary organisation, an area in which she is already deeply involved!

HENRY Headteacher		
Sunday		**Monday**
Slept, woke, dozed.	6–8	7am. Get up with thick head. Shower etc. Off to school.
Coffee and papers in bed. Talked to Mary about our plans. Went for croissants. Breakfast.	8–10	Check diary with secretary. See Bursar. Take Assembly, see 3 staff, 2 boys, 3 phone calls.
Mow lawn, shower. Emergency Governor's meeting.	10–12	Dictate reports and letters General Inspector (Harry) arrives.
Drink in 'The Pig'. Back for lunch with Sally, Steve and grandchildren. Argued with Steve about education policy. He's so stuffy.	12–2	Lunch with Harry and Deputy Heads good to see him again.
Loaded dishwasher and snoozed off after lunch. Played with kids in garden.	2–4	Couple of major problems to deal with.
Tea and TV, continued argument with Steve.	4–6	Year Head's meeting – more phone calls.
Phone calls, Union and Governors on to me.	6–8	Quick sandwich while driving to commitee. Time for quick drink.
Revised old assembly notes in front of telly. Then wrote two staff references.	8–10	Another meeting. Runs late. Drive home at last. Not much longer of this.
John dropped in with bottle of single malt. Really enjoyed it. Bed.	10–12	11pm. Mary and I have a drink and a snack. Read Times Ed. with a glass or two of John's wonderful malt. Bed.

MARY – his wife		
Sunday		**Monday**
Woke at 6.30 as usual, but dozed until about 7.30. Made coffee. Fed cat and dog. Read Sunday papers before Henry woke, took them up to him with coffee.	6-8 8-10	Get up, make coffee. Bath, dress, feed animals. Eat cereal with Henry. Tidy, make beds. Fill washing machine. Read mail.
After breakfast, washed up. Gardened. Prepared roast for lunch, cooked, set table.	10-12	Plan week and meals. Shop.
Sally arrives, drink and chat. Lunch 1.30. Prepare coffee. Play with grandchildren in the garden. Prepare and eat tea. Play snap with grandchildren.	12-2 2-4 4-6	Met Dorothy over lunch. Long talk about new proposals. Discussed lorry leaflet. First draft of lorry leaflet. Print out two campaign letters. Phone calls, tea. Put my feet up and read newspaper.
Clear up. Sort out tomorrow's clothes.	6-8	Chat to Phil and Anne over fence. Spray roses.
Watch play on TV. John arrives to see Henry. Knit. Coffee for self. Tell Henry not to drink too much whisky. Take dog for quick walk. John goes, lock up, bed.	8-10 10-12	Campaign meeting, liked my draft leaflet. Good feedback. Persuade Henry to eat something and help him finish John's malt. Walk dog. Go to bed, read and fall asleep before he comes up.

Your replies to these questions may lead you to re-read the section on Relationships (Chapter 5). Check, too, your Interests and Values.

Mary and Henry are fairly typical of a busy, middle aged, married couple, who probably need to spend more time planning time for each other together. They will also find helpful information in Chapter 8 about health, and particularly Henry's eating and drinking habits.

The diary is a basis from which to decide how you want to plan your time so you can enjoy as much of it as possible.

What to do next: The questions are in two parts. Obviously, if you have already embarked on your life change you will first answer the questions on 'Post-transition Diary'.

Pre-transition Diary

Now

1 How much of the week did you enjoy?

....

2 Did you enjoy those activities you had to do?

....

3 How many of the enjoyable activities were chosen?

....

4 How much time did you spend doing things you dislike?

....

5 Do you choose activities you say you dislike?

....

6 Any significant discoveries?

....

Post-transition Diary

Future

1 What new things will be/are added to your diary?

....

2 What difference could/does this make?

....

3 What will be/is missing from your diary?

....

4 How do you feel about this?

....

5 How will you/do you fill any gaps?

....

6 Will you/do you have all the freedom you need?

....

EXAMPLE

Henry

Now

1 Sunday – most of it, especially the meal. Monday – lunch. Suppose I enjoyed assembly, but I'm ready to give up on the rest.

2 The lunch on Monday, and assembly. Otherwise no!

3 Most of them, See 2.

4 Most of Monday and admin on Sunday evening.

5 Thought this was a stupid question until I realised that I get a lot of satisfaction from being asked advice and making decisions. Maybe I like meetings more than I admit.

6 Didn't realise how regularly I drink but it's probably not important.

Future

1 My role as advisor, more time for reading, more travel. Time for photography, the garden and family.

2 At the moment I am really excited about it although I realise there will be hidden problems.

3 Awkward parents and pupils. Constant governors and union meetings. Cramping the needs into the resources available. Personnel problems.

4 I think I will be better company for Mary and have more time and energy to enjoy the grandchildren.

5 There is no problem with time gaps. I look forward to having more time for research. I'll miss some of my colleagues.

6 Yes I think I will. I'll have to take over some of the things Mary used to do about the house but apart from this I'll be doing what I want to.

EXAMPLE

Mary

Now

1 I enjoy most of my life. Henry has been so busy. I've had to make my own life.

2 Don't enjoy the chores, but they are a part of my job in the house. I like gardening and cooking.

3 Most of them.

4 Watching TV on my own. Trying to fit our social life around Henry's meetings. Recently a fair amount of time, since the children have finally left I have not been satisfied with my life. When we first married we were both teaching and then I was a busy with the children. When that responsibility ended I wasn't quite sure what to do with myself.

6 I'm a bit concerned about Henry's eating habits and he will need to watch his drinking.

Future

1 My mornings will be completely different because I shall be at work. No doubt this will occasionally spill over into my afternoons and evenings. Henry will be home two of the weekday afternoons.

2 It means domestic routine will be completely altered. I used to do things mainly in the morning. Henry will have to do more and I don't think he'll like it. We'll have to make sure we are both not too busy to have time for each other.

3 I'll have to restrict the range of my voluntary activities. And I'll miss my friends dropping in.

4 I'm a little apprehensive about the loss of flexibility and about how Henry and I will get on because we will have a lot more time in the house together.

5 What gaps?

6 Well yes and no. Obviously going to work will eat up my time but I have chosen this. How much free time Henry and I will have after we have finished work and all the household chores depends on how much we allow new commitments to eat into our evenings. Henry in particular.

A diary for one week will not of course cover everything you do with your time. You may prefer another way of time analysis*, to help you consider how you spend your time now, and how you want to spend it in the future.

1 **Committed time:** This is time given to others. There may be choice e.g. as in voluntary work, reward, as in paid employment, no choice e.g. being at school, or in prison.

2 **Fringe time:** Travelling to work; thinking about a meeting while you eat; planning a holiday for yourself and others; walking to the shops through a park.

3 **Care-taking:** Self: Eating, sleeping, washing, dressmaking etc.
Others: Cleaning house, looking after children, listening to friends.

4 **Disposable:** To spend exactly as you like.

EXERCISE 18

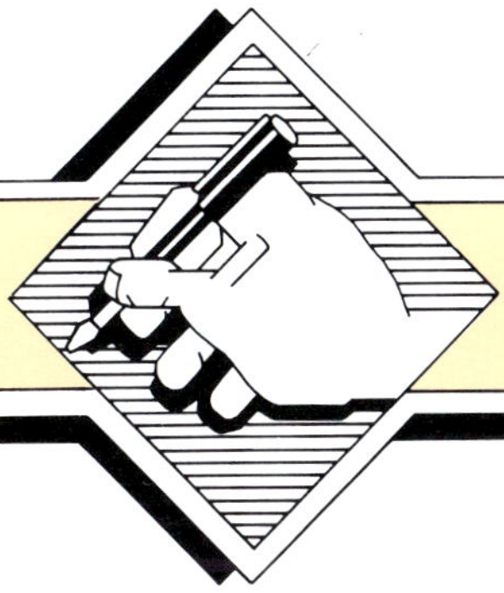

TIME BALANCE SHEET

What to do: Some activities may be in more than one section. It may help if you use a different colour for each section. Include all the areas of your life – work, home, leisure and people.

PRESENT	FUTURE
Committed	
Fringe	
Care	
Disposable	

*Adapted from Barrie Hopson and Mike Scally, Lifeskills Teaching Programmes No. 1

EXAMPLE

Jasmin
A community midwife, lives alone

PRESENT	FUTURE
Committed *Work with mothers and babies. Colleagues. Meetings. Training students. Church, but in my own free time.*	*Nursing Officer, more regular hours so can give more of a regular commitment to Church.*
Fringe *Travel. Shop between phone calls and patients.*	*Far less travel. Shopping easier, close to work.*
Care *Sleep. Gardening. Cooking. Cleaning, shopping. Visiting sick Church members.*	*Need to look a bit smarter. May be able to pay a cleaner.*
Disposable *Gardening. Reading. Church (see committed). Visiting family.*	*Too much. Easier to plan activities as hours are much more regular. Same as before apart from that.*

Jasmin saw that the proportions of her committed and disposable time although changing little in actual numbers of hours would change greatly in their regularity. She expected to get far more satisfaction out of each as a consequence although she will miss the direct contact with babies. She may even lose some disposable time at first because of the need to go on management courses but she will make much better use of what remains.

What To Do Next: Compare your Present balance with the Future balance, and answer these questions:

1 Are you satisfied with the balance now?

2 What, if anything, would you like to change?

3 Is your Future balance very different from the Present?

4 Are you satisfied with the Future balance?

5 How do you plan to make this all happen?

6 Can you plan your time so you are filling all your needs; finances; interests; values; skills; support network? If not, what is still unsatisfactory?

EXAMPLE

Jasmin

1 *Up to a point – there is so much work to do and I find the late hours increasingly tiring.*

2 *I wish I had more time to relax, and to arrange visits to my family.*

3 *Yes, but in quality rather than absolute time. I am going to miss my Mums and babies.*

4 *Oh yes, so far as I can see.*

5 *It will come out of the administrative nature of the new job.*

6 *Yes it will be fine but I will miss the babies.*

Alternative Uses For 'Time Balance Sheet'

1 With your partner

You can use your Time Balance Sheet with your partner, and negotiate ways of spending your joint time together, so that you may each be satisfied with the balance.

2 For self-employment – time in the life of the self-employed

Anyone who is considering self-employment, especially if it means working from home, will discover how much discipline is needed to balance 'work' time and 'personal' time, and to avoid the intrusion of the one upon the other. It is not necessary to plan every minute, or even every week, but it is helpful to know how you spend your time now and to decide what proportion of your time you would like to spend on specific activities.

Use the Balance Sheet to plan a day or week, especially if you work from home and your 'territory' spills over. You may be able to see more clearly where you are using time uneconomically. If you spend more time looking for papers than reading them, you may decide to allocate extra time to develop an effective filing system!

3 The busy person

If your day is full but unsatisfying you seem to be busy but are vaguely bored and frustrated, then make yourself a fresh Balance Sheet or keep a diary for a week.
What exactly were you doing each minute of your day. . . The secret of effective time use is to know what to do NOW. This requires that you know what you want to do, that is, you have worked out the priorities in your life and secondly that you have worked out a timetable for achieving those priorities.
The Time Diary and Time Balance Sheet exercises can be useful for a regular review of your life.
You are now in a position to make definite plans.

PROGRESS 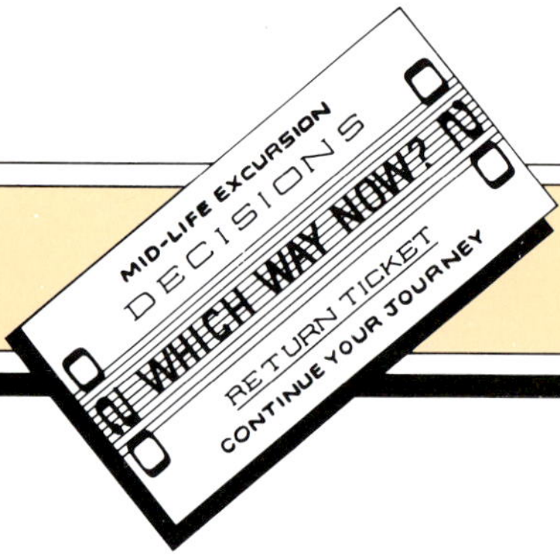 SUMMARY

ANALYSIS AND REVIEW OF:

My interests, values and skills – any additions to comments on Pages 85, 90 and 95.
How I manage my time – my Time Balance Sheet.

IMPORTANT INSIGHTS:

I WANT TO CHANGE:

I WANT TO CONTINUE:

I WANT TO BEGIN, OR TO DEVELOP:

NEW FACTS:

LINKS WITH OTHER PAGES:

WHAT'S NEXT? ON TO:

Practical options: Paid work; job search; part-time work; self-employment.
Unpaid work; leisure opportunities; learning in later life; future life; future patterns of work.

CHAPTER 7

WHAT ARE MY PRACTICAL OPTIONS?

WHAT ARE MY PLANS?
WHAT IS WORK?
HOW DOES IT VARY?

This chapter begins by looking at the different meanings of work. There is a flowchart to help analyse your work options and then a section job search – how to find work in the area you want. There is a section on leisure and returning to learning. By the end of the chapter you will have enough information to make practical plans.

It is common in mid life to reassess priorities. Many of the major events of life have already been experienced; career, marriage, childbirth, parenthood, perhaps divorce and bereavement. We can now evaluate with hindsight what we embarked on with expectation. Also in mid life, structural changes are beginning to occur. Children are growing up and becoming independent, career structures are becoming set, the dependence relationship with our parents is reversing and in late middle age retirement approaches.

So, in this context a review of our attitudes to work is part of a general reassessment of values and priorities occurring in the middle years. Again specific events such as redundancy, separation and retirement will prompt such a review.

What is work? – Who needs it? – How does work vary?

At its most abstract, work can be described as a human interaction with the environment to produce some useful effect. Like all generalisations this description is so broad that it may have little practical use, but it does have one advantage for our review in that it gets away from the idea that work has to mean paid work. Housework, homework, good works, political work, workouts are all types of work which are usually done without any expectation of cash remuneration.

Work needs to be defined more widely than in terms of paid (and possibly unpleasant) employment. Equally it needs to be recognised that paid work is not only the source of social esteem, nor that the lack of paid work implies you are a lesser person (See Chapter 1).

> *You work that you keep pace with the earth, and the soul of the earth. . . .*
> *to love life through labour is to be intimate with life's most inmost secret.*

Khalil Gibran. The Prophet.

> *Absence of occupation is not rest;*
> *A mind quite vacant is a mind distressed.*

Cowper. The Garden.

What kinds of work are there?

Work can be separated into 3 kinds.

1 **Job Work:** Full-time or more or less full-time employment for a wage or salary.

2 **Supplementary Work:** Work which gives less than a full income but which guarantees economic independence. Supplementary work is often done in addition to essential unpaid work, such as housework. It is often done to supplement a partner's income or state benefit.

   The following are some suggestions for supplementary work – probably the most popular form of additional income in the later middle years:

   - Teaching sessional classes in Adult Education (limited unless you have a specific skill)
   - Selling produce of garden or kitchen, to shops, direct to public, or on market stalls
   - Catering industry, especially pubs and hotels
   - Repairing cars, or homes
   - Handicrafts and art
   - Writing/lecturing
   - Childcare

3 **Maintenance Work:** unpaid work done for family, other dependents and the broader community. This includes: housework, DIY, voluntary work, caring, childrearing, etc. This work is essential, much of it is performed by women and traditionally undervalued. Without it society would cease to function. In this group is also included work done for the wider community which is mainly unpaid. Political activity, voluntary activity, community work, local campaigning are examples of such work. Some of them carry high levels of recognition and self esteem.

Depending on your circumstances you could be considering increasing or reducing any of the above, of course your review will involve considering your options within each of the three types.

You may be in work and dissatisfied with your current occupation, or unemployed and looking for work, or seeing your last child on to the school bus and thinking of returning to work. In whichever case, the flowchart on the next page will help you to analyse your future work options.

My Future Work Pattern. . .Flowchart for Decision – Making

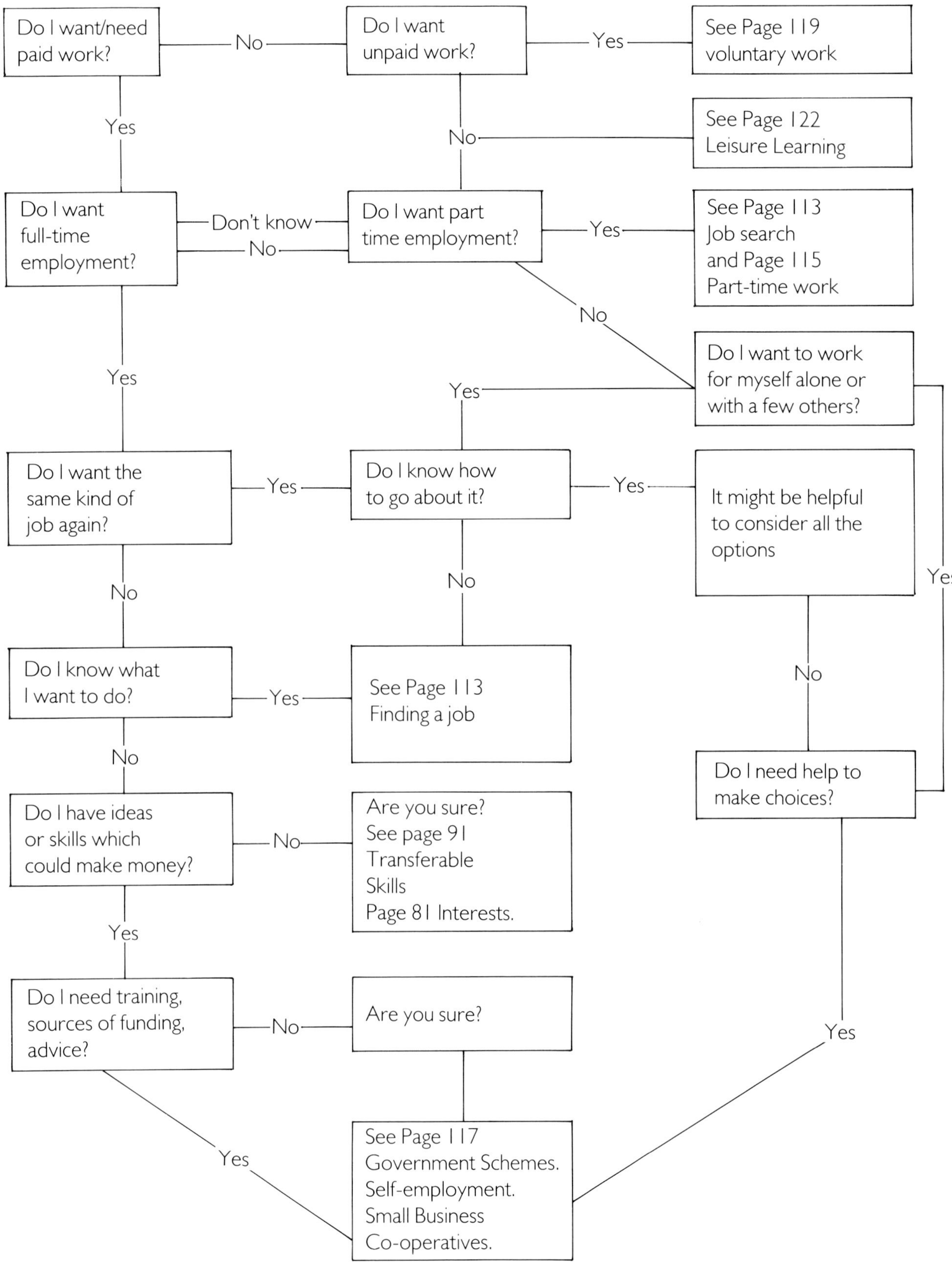

EXAMPLE

FLOWCHART

Martin: 51 **Departmental Manager for Insurance Brokers.** *For the past year I have been helping with the accounts of a local Hospice. I plan to continue this and other work at the Hospice on a voluntary basis, as I find it immensely rewarding. I will have more time available, because the children can now all look after themselves. My wife will continue to teach and our joint income will be the same as before. The Hospice will offer everything I need. I hope to take some training so I can work more closely with the patients and their families. I went straight to Page 119. Voluntary work.*

Rita: 40 **Residential Social Worker.** *I am still wondering whether to take re-training. I have worked in child care for ten years, and I am exploring all possible options. As a widow I need to earn and I want a satisfying job using my administration and caring skills. The flowchart led me to training advice on Page 118.*

Jeanette: 50 **Catering for business people.** *I chose two directions on the flowchart, as I still don't know whether I want to work full or part-time and I saw clearly that there are far more sources of help, advice and re-training than I realised. I'm going to contact my local Polytechnic and the Small Firms Services.*

Job Search. . . Looking for a Paid Job? Full-time or Part-time?

For once changes in the job market are working to the benefit of more mature people. The relative decline in the numbers of young people coming out of school and college means that increasingly employers have to look to other people to fill their vacancies. That said there still remains the extra difficulties of finding a new job in your middle years. You will need to be systematic in your approach but if you have skills and experience to offer, age is not the barrier it once was. Generally part-time work will be easier to find as this is where demand has expanded in recent years. And of course regional variations are still very important.

Where To Look

Obviously the Job Centre and PER (Professional and Executive Register – 32 offices over the country); they will send you *Executive Post.*

Daily and Sunday newspapers; Trade Journals; Professional publications; Employment Recruitment Agencies.

But. . . . only 25% of jobs are found through direct application. . . . only 50% of jobs are advertised.

Remember an employer will employ the most *suitable* candidate, *not* the most *needy* one.

Marketing Yourself

You must let people know you are available for work.

Which People? **Everyone you can think of!**

The 'Old Boy/Girl Network'; people from pubs, clubs, church, college, friends and ex-colleagues, family, neighbours, Unions and Professional Associations, Agencies.

Do not ask them for a job - ask for information and advice.
An excellent way to find a new job is to use a 'Referral System'. This is an American concept which is used increasingly by career counsellors in the UK. Everyone likes to be thought an expert, everyone likes to help. No-one enjoys the embarrassment of saying 'No', especially to a friend, so *don't* ask for work, but *do* ask genuinely for ideas; who should you approach, which companies need staff with your skills? Could they suggest the best place to begin your search? Always write to someone you know personally, and follow up your letter with a telephone call. Ask for a brief meeting – and keep it brief – no longer than twenty minutes unless you are specifically asked to stay longer. Make sure you obtain the name of at least one other person you can write to, with the permission of your contact. It may be that your contacts will have work available in the future and will remember you, when they have something concrete to offer.

Your letter can be very straightforward.

> Dear
> As you may have heard, I have decided to leave my present position and find another job, possibly part-time. I am writing to you, as one of the most experienced people in the field, to ask your advice. I do not expect you to have a job available, but I would like to talk briefly to you to see who I might approach and what opportunities might be open to me. I know you are extremely busy and would not expect to take up much of your time.
> I enclose a copy of my C.V. and would be grateful for your comments.
> Yours sincerely,

If you are unused to looking for a job, writing CVs (Short for Curriculum Vitae – career history) and attending interviews, the local Job Centre, Job Club, or a local self-help group may be able to offer you advice, interview practice or help in writing CVs or letters.

There is no harm in replying to advertisments. If you want to check which organisation employs people in your particular field, or to find out details of a company before you go for an interview, go to your Reference Library and look in:

Dun and Bradstreet; Kellys; Kompass; Times Top 5000.

CVs – Personal Information to Circulate

Even if you have an application form for a job, include in your reply a copy of your CV. When you are replying to advertisements, or writing to people you have never met, send a CV with your letter. Send a copy to contacts you *do* know, and ask for their comments. Your CV should have your name and full address at the top, and should be printed or well-typed. Prospective employers are interested in what you want to *do*; proof that you can do it; what you have *been* doing and what you have to offer them. Personal details and educational qualifications can go at the end.

	Terence O'Neil 7 The Avenue, Newton, W7 Telephone No. 12345 678
Objectives:	(Type of work you are looking for). Marketing post in small company, possibly with foreign travel, preferably in the field of engineering equipment.
Experience:	25 years as marketing manager in major company. Three years as trainee sales engineer, based in Madrid.
Achievements:	Sold more machines than any other company in the field. Increased profits most years. Trained staff in my department for past 10 years. Awards for reports of customer satisfaction. Fluent Spanish, some German.
Employers:	(Give names of employer(s), with your job title and responsibilities in each role – beginning with the most recent. Put *dates* at the *right–hand side*).
Finally, give them some information which will say something about your general interests and educational background.	
Education:	Newton Grammar School BSc Engineering 1959 Marketing and Management Courses
Interests:	Photography, climbing, travel
Personal:	Married. Age 52. Two married children. Excellent health.

Part-time Work

A part–time job may be your ideal solution. It should fulfill the need to earn and also offer time for leisure interests or other responsibilities. For employers there is often an advantage in employing part-time labour, and age may be less of a barrier when looking for part-time employment.

People with specific skills – accountancy, nursing, teaching, may be able to do freelance work. If you have a practical service to offer, try advertising in your local newspaper or shops. It may be worth paying for a printed handout to send to local organisations, describing what you do – and use the Referral System!

Freelance part-time work may be very spasmodic. Unless you are offered regular work – perhaps one day a week, or one week each month – you will find it useful to decide roughly what you want to earn and how often you want to work.

All this information applies to the next section, on self-employment.

Beware The Myth of Self-Employment Part-Time Work!

Self-Employment

The numbers of self-employed people continue to rise by around 30% annually and there is a great deal of encouragment – practical, cash, information, advice etc., from both government and business interests. Rank Xerox and ICI were among the larger employers who first encouraged their staff to move their offices into the home by giving them the technology and a guaranteed number of days' work. Thus they have a gradual, supported entry to the world of full self-employment; some financial security while they find other clients and expand their consultancies, and the companies are saving on overheads. Other companies followed this example. In the UK, at least 10,000 new businesses are registered every month, **but**:

- 25% disappear within a year.
- Up to 40% fail in the first three years.

If you are attracted to the idea of working for youself, either alone or by setting up a small company, and if the information from your self-analysis reinforces your thinking, consider the following points:

THIS.		OR THIS?
I have enough permanent income to allow me to experiment.	–	I might squander my capital if I don't seek sound advice.
It is far less risky than when I was younger, and had more dependents.	–	I might get depressed if I don't achieve immediately, then take stupid risks.
Being independent, my own boss.	–	Having complete responsibility for everything.
Time for *all* my interests.	–	No time for any other life.
Working the hours I choose.	–	Working long and unsocial hours.
Only doing things I enjoy.	–	Persuading others to buy my goods or services.
Doing *everything* myself, no need to rely on others.	–	Being my own filing clerk, etc.
Working from home, everything available when needed.	–	Mixing home with work and doing neither thoroughly.
Working from home, tax deductable expenses.	–	No fringe benefits (paid holiday or sick pay; private medicine; company perks).

If you are still enthusiastic, go ahead, as long as you have
STAMINA. . . A SENSE OF HUMOUR. . . OPTIMISM. . .
SUPPORTIVE FAMILY AND FRIENDS
AND A HIGHLY MARKETABLE IDEA!

Remember that no-one owes you a living, you will have to convince people they need you rather than someone else. Fewer than half of self-employed people cite money as their main motive but you are in business to make profits. . . no matter how small. If you are to survive, you will need to earn more than you spend, eventually, if not in the early stages.

It is helpful to make a written plan stating:

1 Why you want to work for yourself.
2 What goods or services you intend to provide.
3 What evidence you have that there is a market.
4 How you propose to trade (sole trader, partnership, company, from home, from premises etc.).

When you are clear about your ideas, take them to someone who can give advice, you will find help easily:

STARTUP – Your Own Business – Open University

The objective of this programme is to help people turn ideas into successful commercial ventures, encouraging the establishment of small firms with well thought out plans and training. This should decrease the enormously high number of bankruptcies or failures.

Students prepare a business plan to present to a panel of business experts, and are allocated a personal adviser for nine months.

STARTUP is not cheap, but could prove a very sound investment.

For more details, write to: Associate Student Central Office
Open University
P O Box 76
Milton Keynes MK7 6AN

Other Sources of Help for the Self-Employed

Small Firms Centres:	FREEFONE 2444 for the address of the nearest one. They offer general business information, training, individual advice and counselling. Advice on marketing, *administration, loans – much of it free.
Enterprise Agencies:	Ask for address of the nearest agency at the Job Centre or PER. They can act as brokers between people with ideas and organisations with funds. They also offer the same kinds of advice and help as Small Firms Centres.
RDC:	Rural Development Commission. Equivalent of Small Firms Centres for those living in the country.

Again DO seek advice – rules may change

Enterprise Allowance

You may qualify for the Enterprise Allowance Scheme: This would give you an income of £40 weekly for one year.

The qualifying conditions are:

1. You must have been registered unemployed *and eligible for benefits* for at least 8 weeks. Some older married women who have not been paying full N.I. contributions have been unable to obtain the Enterprise Allowance for the small business they had planned.
2. You must be over 18.
3. You must have £1,000 available to invest in the business before you begin (this can be a bank loan).
4. You must be prepared to work full time in the business.
5. The business must be new and independent.
6. If you have partners, you may each qualify for the £40 weekly – and must each have £1,000 available.
7. Applicants are required to attend a free one-day training course to ensure awareness of pitfalls.

Among some of the schemes authorised are:

- Breeding racing pigeons.
- A singing telegram firm.
- Repairing musical instruments.
- Dress shops.
- Human relations consultants.

There are several specialist journals for small businesses. Also there are a vast number of books available on setting up and running a small business, with new titles coming out weekly.

*See Chapter 10 for further addresses.

Co-operatives
Co-operatives are businesses which are owned and controlled by the members. The movement is expanding and diverging dramatically, from fewer than 50 in 1971 to around 1600 today and growing at the rate of 40 each week. In the past, co-operatives tended to be very small, to be formed by young people and to cover wholefood distribution, printing, crafts and similar products, although the co-operative movement began originally with the Rochdale Pioneers.

Although it is dangerous to generalise, co-operatives are often small, with five-ten members. It is essential to be confident that the teamwork will last, enjoy sharing ideas and work, and dispensing with hierarchies. The co-operatives movement is expanding. If you would like more information, the Open University has produced a pack on co-operatives. There is now a National Co-operative Development Agency, and many areas now have Co-operative Development Workers. See Page 165.

Financial Assistance and training

There are many schemes for funding new enterprises, but as the Government projects and funding change rapidly, get the most up-to date information from your Job Centre, the Small Firms Service or Enterprise agency. You will also find helpful details in some of the books listed on Pages 161 and 162.
There are a number of government training schemes designed to cater for adults who, for any reason, need a training course in order to seek re-employment. As these schemes change regularly, ask for information from your Job Centre. The Training Agency (formerly the Manpower Services Commission) may be able to offer retraining and there may also be Open College programmes – again, ask the relevant agencies.

Other Assistance
It is advisable to talk to one of the agencies already mentioned. Practical help may be available locally, in the form of loans of tools or premises, cheap materials, printing facilities, etc.

Self-Help Groups
There is a national network of self-help groups for the unemployed and there are several centres specifically for older people. The Job Change Project in Birmingham was set up for over–40s, and the Third Age Project in Totnes is for over–45s who are retired or unemployed. There may be similar projects where you live, or you could help to set one up.
The initative for one scheme came from John Laidlaw, a businessman who had retired early. The intention is to earn money through marketing crafts and other products. The older members would support and offer their marketing skills to the younger, thus giving them experience in running a small business and increasing their independence. You could find out more by contacting John Laidlaw direct at Valley House, Little Baddow Road, Woodham Walter, Maldon, Essex. It might be a way of replacing work satisfactions, including meeting younger people.

You can get more information about self-help groups from B.U.R.N. (British Unemployment Resources Network), 319, Summer Lane, Newton, Birmingham, B19.

Unpaid Work

This section covers working as a volunteer, with no financial gain, other than expenses, for a voluntary agency. It does not cover all maintainance work.

How Do I Choose? Type Of Work? Time I Spend?
Approach your decision as if it were a paid job. Use the information you have acquired about your skills, interests, values and the way you want to spend your time. Search out the kind of work you will find most satisfying.
If you take on work you dislike, or are persuaded to give more time than you had intended, you will be less effective both with the clients and the agency. Finding the work that is best for *you* will be mutally beneficial.

You don't *have* to work in a hospital, or with large groups of people, or be chatty and friendly! You could use your 'job skills', be an accountant for a small voluntary organisation, teach young unemployed people your own skills, be a shopkeeper for Oxfam. Provided you are fit, you might travel for a year in the Third World, working for VSO, as they are interested in older people with skills which are essential to developing countries.

It makes sense to utilise the energies and expertise of a group of highly experienced and mature people whose financial position enables them to provide their services free. There are also schemes whereby the larger companies second experienced staff to voluntary agencies, paying their salaries whilst the agency uses their services. The voluntary agency benefits from skills it could not otherwise afford. There is a danger in the suggestion that volunteers could do work that might, perhaps, be made into paid jobs. The reality of cuts in public expenditure, changes in the age balance of the population and no return to full employment in the forseeable future, creates a need for volunteers. Even when the public sector employed far more workers, voluntary organisations were an essential part of the community. Although fears have been expressed about the increasing use of volunteers, they rarely replace paid workers. Without volunteers, many areas of social need would be without help of *any kind.*

Where Do I Look For Voluntary Work?

There is Volunteer Bureau in most towns. The magazine New Statesman & Society has a weekly 'Volunteer Noticeboard', where agencies advertise for helpers, specifying the kind of work available. If you do not want to buy the magazine, the reference room of your public library will have a copy.

Some ideas:

REACH – Retired Executives Active Clearing House (See page 166).
Arranges part or full time voluntary jobs in your area of expertise
Tries to match the volunteer to the job and the district, so you may have to wait several months

MIND – Mental Health

Disabled Living Foundation

National Careers Association

Oxfam

Adult Literacy

Friends of hospitals and friends of hospice

Citizens Advice Bureau

Save the Children Fund

(You will find addresses and suggestions for further reading in Chapter 10.)

Many voluntary agencies offer training of a high standard to their volunteers, for example, the Samaritans, Relate, formerly the National Marriage Guidance Council and the Citizens Advice Bureau, whose workers are trained to professional standards.

Voluntary work is seen by Alvin Toffler, in *The Third Wave,* as part of the return to 'community-building'.

> *Older people in every community could be appointed adjunct, teachers or mentors, invited to teach some of their skills in local schools... under school supervision, retired photographers could teach photography...*

Even if schools are reluctant to use non-teachers, and some of them already have arrangements for such help, there is always work of this kind with the unemployed school-leaver.

Pressure Groups

If you are, or become, a member of organisations like the Patients Association, the National Trust, Amnesty International, CND, which pursue your interests and attempts to change public opinion, you can work for them. There is always office work, fundraising, publicity. If you are supporting a pressure group, attendance at meetings is work in itself! There are several pressure groups covering the needs of older people.

Leisure – What is it? How to get the most from it?

Attempts at defining leisure are by and large unsatisfactory because there is always something that does not fit the definition. A way round this dilemma is to say that leisure is what we do in leisure time. Leisure time is that time in which we are not engaged in income earning or maintenance activities. Maintenance activities are those essential non-paid activities which we do for ourselves and those about us e.g. cooking, shopping, washing, cleaning, etc. We then have a three fold division of our time into:

*Sold Time: the time we do our earning and its related activities ie. school.
Maintenance Time: time used for essential non paid activities eg. sleeping, eating and those given above.
Leisure Time: the rest of our time left over from sold time and maintenance time.

This way of looking at leisure makes it clear that the amount of leisure time available will vary greatly from individual to individual, because each of us differs in how much of the day we spend on sold time and maintenance time. Of course we could choose to increase our leisure time by reducing sold time and accepting a lower income. Equally we can increase leisure time by doing our maintenance tasks more efficiently and thereby reducing maintenance time. These are exactly the sorts of areas we should be looking at in our mid-life review.

Assuming that we have balanced our priorities to give ourselves the maximum leisure time in the circumstances, how do we get the best of our leisure time?

Look back at Chapter 5 and draw up two lists under the following headings:

How I spend my leisure time NOW (list activities and times spent per week.)	How I would like to spend my leisure time (list activities and allocate time for each.)

If your lists are the same you are making the best use of your leisure time. But if they differ you could get more satisfaction out of your leisure time by increasing the proportion of time spent on the under-represented activities. Identify these and plan them into your routine.

> *Increased means and increased leisure are the two civilisers of man. . .*
>
> Benjamin Disraeli

How can I expand my leisure interests?
In life as in art 'I know what I like' often means 'I like what I know'. But as old activities become jaded or lose their relevance it is important to replace them with new activities if we are to avoid television expanding into every minute of our spare time. Fortunately we live at a time when the variety and opportunity for leisure activity is expanding as never before. The problem now is not what to do but how to find out about it.

* These ideas are explored fully in the Lifeskills book 'Conquer the Clock' Time Management NOW.

Public libraries offer a wealth of information about opportunities in your own locality. Community Centres, Local Education Authorities and Town Halls can also help.
Advertising in the local and national press carry lots of information about leisure pursuits. Many papers also publish a 'What's on' guide.
For useful books and addresses of organisations which offer leisure activities, see Chapter 10.
It is often difficult to separate 'Leisure' from 'Learning', but education is considered separately in Exercise 19.
There are so many opportunities for leisure activities that only a very brief selection is possible. The ideas below are for unusual ways of enjoying your leisure, which you may not have considered.

Art:
How about becoming a 'Friend' of your nearest major Art Gallery? Not only will it be cheaper to go to exhibitions, but you could be invited to private views, specialist lectures, and to use restaurant or other facilities.
Become a practitioner, not just at local adult education classes, but on painting or pottery holidays; lace-making, wood-carving or other crafts.

Environment:
If you enjoy the countryside, or are concerned about pollution or the preservation of wild life, you can join various organisations, from the National Trust to Friends of the Earth. Interested in organic farming? Try WWOOF! Working Weekends on Organic Farms where you can spend an unusual and healthy weekend helping on an organic farm and eating delicious food. If you have no garden but enjoy growing things, you could share an allotment with a friend, if a whole allotment seems too large for your needs. There are also Adult Education classes for gardeners.

Music:
Like Art Galleries, Opera companies have 'Friends' who can buy tickets at a discount – and as priority, or attend dress rehearsals. You could learn to play an instrument or join a music appreciation class.

Physical Activity:
Become a coach! Take up cycling. Outdoor Pursuits Centres have special programmes for older people. Stay healthy, take regular exercise and enjoy it too!

Travel:
The Greater London Association for Pre-retirement information booklet 'Holiday', has 40 very detailed pages of information ranging from Disabled Person's Railcard to warnings about lack of bath plugs in Russia. An excellent buy!

These suggestions are just tasters, leisure can be hard work!

> *Wo/man ultimately decides for him/herself and in the end, education must be towards the ability to decide.*

Victor Frankl

You may have studied for qualifications, to pass examinations, or attended recreational classes. You may even think your education ended the day you left school, especially if the experience was unpleasant. If most of *your* education was acquired outside the world of school and college, you may hesitate to return to study.

Adults often fear they will be unable to absorb information, or be unwelcome among the younger students.

Extract from a letter from Alan George, Course Tutor, Learning in Later Life Programme, Polytechnic of North London, July 1985

"I find myself asking what it is that attracts and holds the enthusiasm of this older student population. They are not seeking qualifications – either academic or professional, although a few retired people have gone on to study for degrees on the Polytechnic's full-time programme. Their motivation is generally rather different and can best be illustrated anecdotally. One woman has a keen interest in history, which started at school, but which had been fairly latent through the busy years of bringing up a family.
Now she and her husband are studying in a building which they previously only knew from the outside. They thought that the Polytechnic was for young students working for degrees – an opportunity which had passed them by. Diffident about responding to the publicity for a course for older people, first the wife, then some three years later, the husband, were persuaded through personal contact that they could not only enter the building, but enjoy lectures and discussion groups, using the library and other facilities of a large higher education institution. The members of our programme enjoy proximity with younger students and the bustle of a large college, although they also value the company of their peers. . . . tutors remark on the spontaneity and participation of older students who bring a lifetime's experience to discussions."

Why return to learning?

- To enjoy it
- To widen horizons and gain new experience
- To change your attitudes or behaviour
- To develop new ideas – and in relation to others
- To pass examinations or clarify thinking.

The next exercise will enable you to see what might be stopping you!

EXERCISE 19

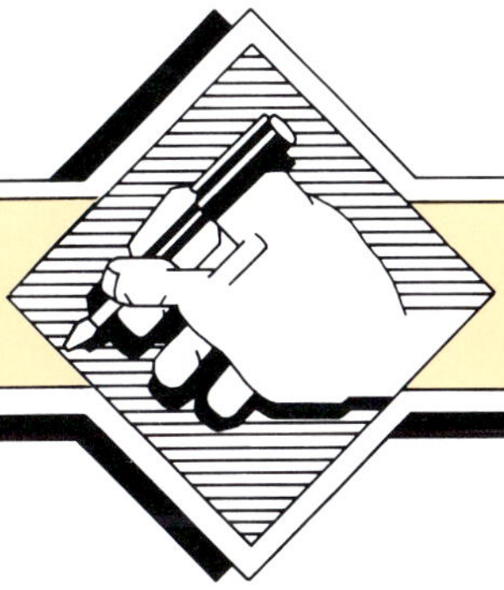

REDISCOVERING LEARNING – MY ATTITUDES

What to do: Complete the sentences. If you are uncertain how to end each one, ask other people what they think about – particularly their own! As you remember your schooldays, you will probably see that any unfortunate experiences need no longer affect you!

1 Learning is ....

....

2 When I left school, I thought..

....

3 My experience of learning was ....

....

4 The best thing about school was ....

....

5 The thing I liked least about school was..

....

6 Since I left school, my experience of learning has been ....

....

7 I would like to learn ....

....

8 People like me don't..

....

9 Mature people can't..

....

10 I would feel .... about studying....................................

....

What To Do Next: Take courage, if you need it! Use the information below and in Chapter 10. More addresses are given in the same chapter.

1 Higher education – degree, diploma or general study

Contact: Local Education Authority or direct to University or Polytechnic. Lists of subjects etc. in public library.

2 Local Adult Education – practical; short courses; creative

Contact: Your Local Authority (in the phonebook under your City, Borough or County Council) or contact the College or institution directly.

3 Study from home – includes all the previously mentioned

Contact: Open University. See page 162. There is a one week Summer School which is residential. The OU offers smaller projects and Community Education as well as degrees. It was originally intended to attract people who had had no opportunity to study full time. Although the OU offers courses by correspondence, you also have a tutor and a local centre.

National Extension College, Cambridge offers self study and tutor assisted courses and materials on a range of subjects, some leading to national qualifications.

Open College. Offers courses on a range of subjects, often vocationally related and some leading to national qualifications. You can choose to study with or without tutor support. Costs vary accordingly.

This final extract, from a letter to the *Guardian* confirms the delight of returning to learning:

> *"I would like to join the discussion aroused by the recent article (April 22) on the anguish of "being over 50". The respondent who described her new-found joy in returning to study is typical of a growing number of people who find new interest and stimulation in learning in later life.*
>
> *I am in daily contact with hundreds of older adults who are students in this polytechnic who have found a whole new world opening up for them through learning. The route for many of them takes the form of an initial counselling session at our guidance unit (Educational Guidance for Adults), then to a preparation course to acquaint older students with study methods, to give them an opportunity to find out if they like to study by actually making a start, then possibly following this by becoming an associate student, testing the water by putting one toe in, and taking one subject from a degree programme, then eventually making an informed choice to enrol on either a part-time or a full-time degree.*
>
> *This Polytechnic (like others) considers it has a special responsibility to provide continuing education routes for older adults who may never have tasted the joy of study. The rewards for staff are beyond measure."*
>
> *Ruth Michael, Hatfield Polytechnic.*

PROGRESS SUMMARY

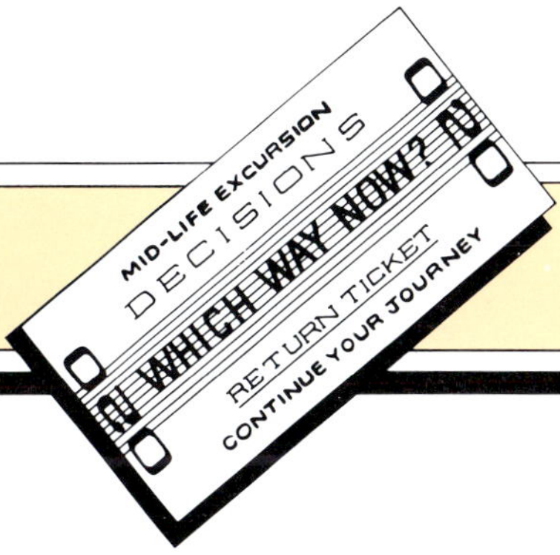

ANALYSIS AND REVIEW OF:

Work – paid and unpaid.
Leisure.
Learning.

IMPORTANT INSIGHTS:

I WANT TO CHANGE:

I WANT TO CONTINUE:

I WANT TO BEGIN, OR TO DEVELOP:

NEW FACTS:

LINKS WITH OTHER PAGES:

WHAT'S NEXT? ON TO:
Taking Care of Myself Health – Stress Management – Personal Health Contract.

CHAPTER 8

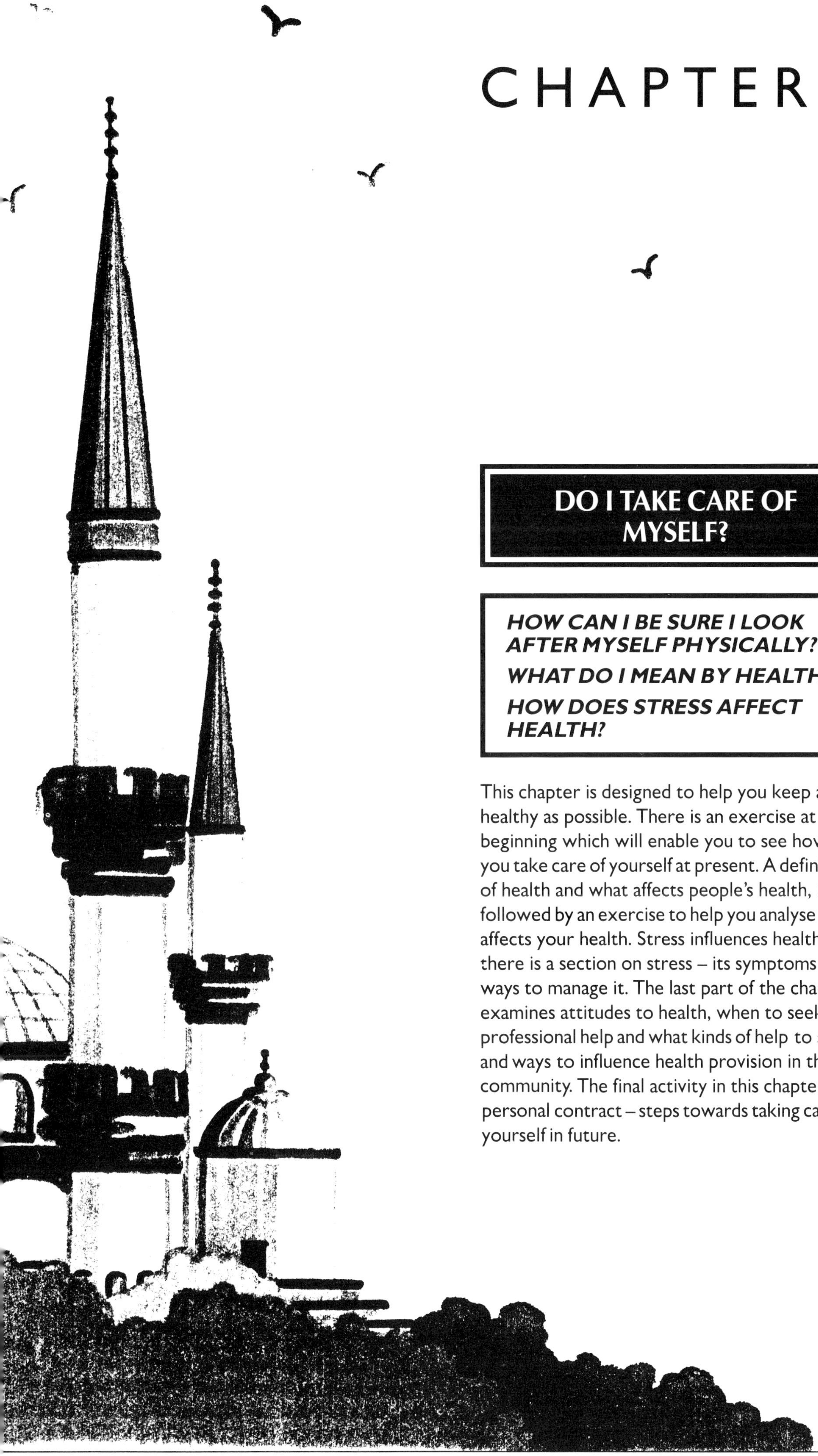

DO I TAKE CARE OF MYSELF?

HOW CAN I BE SURE I LOOK AFTER MYSELF PHYSICALLY?

WHAT DO I MEAN BY HEALTH?

HOW DOES STRESS AFFECT HEALTH?

This chapter is designed to help you keep as healthy as possible. There is an exercise at the beginning which will enable you to see how well you take care of yourself at present. A definition of health and what affects people's health, is followed by an exercise to help you analyse what affects your health. Stress influences health, and there is a section on stress – its symptoms and ways to manage it. The last part of the chapter examines attitudes to health, when to seek professional help and what kinds of help to seek and ways to influence health provision in the community. The final activity in this chapter is a personal contract – steps towards taking care of yourself in future.

> *With me, health means keeping up my accustomed way of living, without discomfort.*
>
> Montaigne.

Not a lecture on illness – nor an injunction to jog!

It is difficult nowadays to walk into a newsagent, or open a magazine, without reading advice on becoming fitter, more beautiful, or slimmer. If you would like to find out more about specific activities, or help you may need, there are lists of books and addresses of specialist organisations in Chapter 10. *The Open University Good Health Guide* offers an excellent and entertaining comprehensive study of all aspects of health. Looking after yourself physically and mentally is vital to the maintenance of health. The leitmotif of this book has been the close relationship between change, stress and health. You have been reflecting on the ways you manage change in your own life, on the people, places and activities which offer you satisfaction, and on your practical needs so that you may plan a rewarding future.

The next two exercises will enable you to judge how well you are taking care of yourself, to see where you learned your attitudes to health, and to decide where you might want to make changes.

EXERCISE 20 — TAKING CARE OF MYSELF

What to do: Circle the number in the relevant column beside each item. Add up your score for each section.

	Always	Nearly Always	Some – times	Rarely	Never
A FOOD					
1 I eat regular meals. Usually 3 a day.	5	4	3	2	1
2 I eat a balanced diet – proteins, vitamins, fibre.	5	5	3	1	1
3 My weight is about average for my height and age.	5	5	3	1	1
4 My digestion is excellent.	5	5	3	1	1
5 My bowels and bladder function satisfactorily.	5	4	3	1	1
SUBTOTAL A					
B DRINK					
6 I drink at least three pints of water daily (including tea & coffee).	5	5	3	2	1
7 I drink half a pint of milk daily (no more than a pint).	5	4	3	2	1
8 I drink no more than 2 pints of beer or 2 measures of spirits or wine daily.	5	4	2	1	1
SUBTOTAL B					

	Always	Nearly Always	Some – times	Rarely	Never
C SMOKING					
9 I am a non-cigarette smoker.	5	3	1	1	1
10 I am a non-pipe smoker.	5	3	3	1	1
11 I am a non-cigar smoker.	5	3	3	1	1
SUBTOTAL C					
D EXERCISE					
12 I walk at least two miles daily.	5	5	3	2	2
13 I do keep fit exercise (ten minutes) daily.	5	5	3	3	1
14 I take part in games or sport.	5	5	3	2	2
15 I swim regularly.	5	5	4	2	2
16 I carry out 'normal' household activities:					
a) Cleaning	5	5	3	2	1
b) Gardening	5	5	3	2	1
c) Climbing Stairs	5	5	3	1	1
SUBTOTAL D					
E RECHARGING THE BATTERIES					
17 I average 7 hours sleep each night.	5	5	3	2	2
18 I sleep fewer hours but feel refreshed.	5	4	3	1	1
19 I spend time in fresh air.	5	4	3	1	1
20 I spend time in gardens or country.	5	4	3	2	1
21 I practise yoga.	5	4	4	2	2
22 I practise meditation.	5	4	4	2	2
23 I practise relaxation.	5	4	4	1	1
24 I practise deep breathing.	5	4	3	1	1
25 I have a spiritual faith.	5	4	3	2	2
26 I plan time to do 'nothing'.	5	5	3	2	1
27 I take holidays.	5	5	3	2	1
SUBTOTAL E					
F PEOPLE					
28 I have close relationships.	5	4	3	1	1
29 I have casual friendships.	5	5	3	2	1
30 I have friends and neighbours.	5	5	3	2	1
31 I have a sexual relationship.	5	5	3	2	2
32 I am willing to talk about bad times.	5	5	3	2	2
33 I can ask for support.	5	4	3	2	1
34 I have stimulating conversations.	5	5	3	2	1
SUBTOTAL F					
G INTERESTS					
35 I have interests which offer mental stimulus.	5	5	3	2	1
36 I have interests which allow me to learn new skills.	5	5	3	2	1
37 I follow current events – media, newspapers.	5	5	3	2	1
38 I have relaxing interests.	5	5	3	2	1
39 I give myself treats.	5	5	3	2	1
40 I take care of my appearance.	5	5	3	1	1
SUBTOTAL G					

What to do next: How to interpret your score:

Overall score:	186–210	Excellent-if you were totally honest!
	151–185	Good; how can you make it even higher?
	101–150	Some way to go–look carefully at each sub-total, to see where you can improve.
	50–100	You are at risk–you may need help from some professional source.

Sub-totals	There may be immediate action you can take which will improve your self-care in a specific area. There is more detailed information about each section in Chapter 10.
FOOD:	If you scored below 20, do you need to change the kind of food you eat, the time you eat it, the amount?
DRINK:	If you scored below 9, you may like to look more closely at your drinking patterns and the cause.
SMOKING:	If you score below 10–no comment.
EXERCISE:	If you score below 20, make a serious attempt to take more exercise. Start gently, either brief warm-up exercises, walking or swimming.
RECHARGING THE BATTERIES:	If you scored less than 40, you may be rather too tense or anxious. Find some regular way of relaxing.
PEOPLE:	If you scored below 20, take another look at Exercise 9, My Personal Network. If you are a naturally reserved or shy person, read the example; other people may be shy too!
INTERESTS:	If you scored 14, you may want to plan more stimulating activities. A low score of 39 and 40 may be an indication of low self esteem, especially if it is combined with a low score in the 'People' section.

After you have digested the information in rest of the chapter, you will have an opportunity to set yourself goals for changes in your lifestyle, in the form of a Personal Contract, rather like New Year resolutions.

What is health?

> *Health is that state of mental, moral and physical well-being which enables people to face any crisis in life with the utmost felicity and grace.*

Pericles.

Perceptions of and attitudes towards health are intensely individual, and Pericles' definition needs no expansion.

Health is more than the absence of illness. Nor is it *entirely* the product of positive attitudes and keeping fit.

External Health Hazards

There are social, economic and enviromental factors which create health hazards. Overcrowding, low income, poor housing, poor diet, noise, pollution and boring, repetitious work all influence health.
So do too many refined foods and the abuse of socially acceptable drugs like tobacco and alcohol. Too little exercise or mental stimulus and too few social contacts constitute health risks.

Although some things, like eyesight, automatically deteriorate with age, age alone is neither a symptom, nor a cause, of ill-health.

In the same way that many mothers are told that their baby's temperature, or rash, is due to teething, so many worrying conditions in older people are often dimissed as 'Your age, my dear', as though age itself is an illness of some kind! You will know if you have indications of new and unusual symptoms, and you have the right to an answer which looks beyond your date of birth!

Your own health patterns, which are a product of your life-experience, have probably been established for many years. It is always possible to change attitudes and behaviour, and an understanding of the origins of those attitudes helps to create new ones if you want to.

The next exercise offers you the opportunity to examine your own attitudes to health, by completing a Health Profile.

EXERCISE 21

MY HEALTH PROFILE

What to do: Answer the questions which are designed to show you how you define health, in other people and in yourself, and what has influenced your attitudes.

1 The healthiest person I know is ...., because ....

2 At present, I am .... healthy.

3 As a small child, my health was affected by ....

4 The messages I have been given about health (e.g. 'Headaches get you attention': or 'Never go out in the rain': 'Illness is unnecessary', etc) include ....

....

5 As a young adult, my health was affected by ....

6 In general, my health has been affected by ....

7 If I retire early, my health will ....

8 The main areas where I need to take care are ....

....

9 In ten years time I might be concerned about ....

....

10 Nowadays, my health is affected by ....

....

11 In order to stay healthy, I ....

....

12 Other people who are affected by my state of health are ....

....

13 When I have problems with health, I am helped by talking to ....

....

14 My score for Taking Care of Myself was ....

15 I need to examine my attitude to ....

....

16 Major life events which have affected my health are ....

....

17 I would seek professional help about ....

18 Doctors always ....

19 My experience of hospitals is ....

20 If I need information about my health, I will ....

....

What to do next: Reflect on your answers, and discuss them with someone who knows you well.

Then answer the questions below.

1 What did you discover about your attitudes to health?

....

....

2 What connections are there between your early history and your present health?

....

....

3 How has this exercise helped you? ....

....

4 As a result of this exercise, what action do you intend to take? ....

....

EXAMPLE

Nita Purchasing Manager

1 *I suppose the most amusing discovery was in the messages. I could hear my grandmother saying, "Don't tread in puddles, you'll catch cold", and my mother saying "Eat it up, it will do you good". I've always had a weight problem! I realised my 'health' affects my temper, and therefore my family, my staff and my colleagues! The menopause has made me very irritable, but it's improving. Also I realised cold and damp lower my spirits and my energy, along with the pressure from my job. I shall have to take positive steps to avoid stress.*

2 *I was a 'chesty child', and that got worse when we came to Britain. I always get bad chest colds when there's a crisis. I lost my voice when I started my first job. It's only since I've been working through this book that I've made such a close connection. The major event which affected my early life was the death of my father. I get ill when there is a major crisis.*

3 *I am now fully aware that promotion is a major event too! I intend to take good care of myself and to live to 100. My main concern is about losing my independence, being physically or mentally infirm, so I only want to be 100 if I can walk to my birthday party (and perhaps even make the cake, who knows?) It made me aware how lucky I am. I don't go to the doctor very often, and I've only been to hospital for my tonsils and to have my first baby. My doctor was very kind when I had hepatitis, but they aren't always patient with minor symptoms, and they do seem to give a lot of drugs. My daughter went to an osteopath for an aching wrist. She says health visitors have been very helpful to her, and sometimes the chemist.*

4 *I'll have to be careful about my weight and my chest (wrap up warm is another of my grandmothers messages). I shall find someone to walk regularly with. It will help me stick to my plan! I shall eat regular meals and cut down on biscuits!*

AGEING – ATTITUDES – HEALTH – MYTHS:

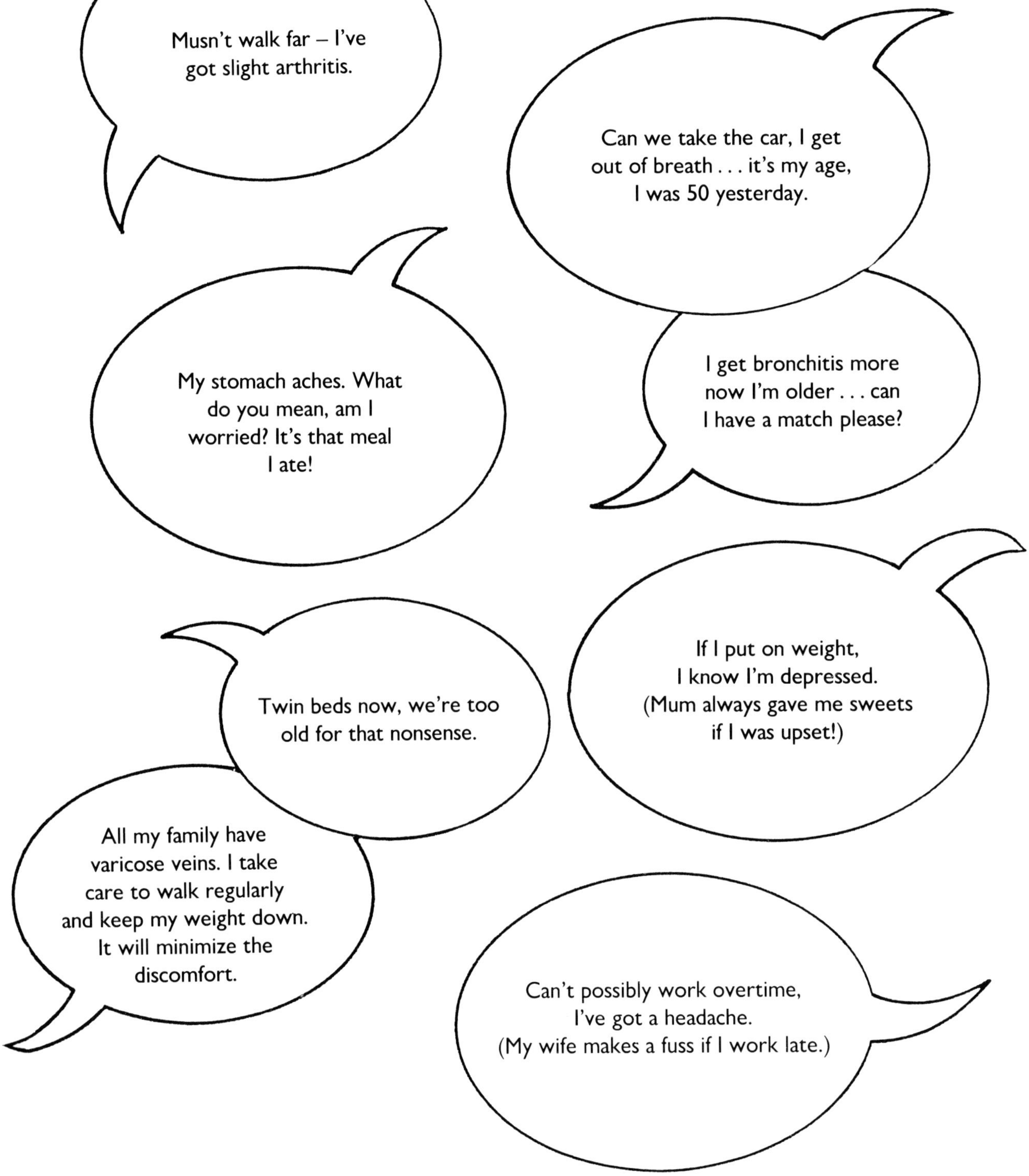

How do my attitudes and thoughts affect my health?

There are certain characteristics which deteriorate with age, see Chapter 4, but limitations are often influenced by attitudes and lifetime habits. If older people become ill, the speed of their recovery depends to a large extent on their attitudes, their confidence and their general well-being. Such comments may seem to suggest that if you feel unwell, somehow you are responsible. Psychosomatic illness is sometimes interpreted as "You're doing it on purpose!" or imagining the symptoms. Of course everyone feels unwell at times, and throughout this book you have been learning of the increased vulnerability to illness of people who are under a great deal of stress.

If stress affects health, how can I prevent or minimise my own stress?

What is stress?

> *Everybody has it, everbody talks about it yet few people have taken the trouble to find out what stress really is . . . Nowadays, we hear a great deal at social gatherings about the stress of executive life, retirement, exercise, family problems, pollution, air traffic control, or the death of a relative . . . The word 'stress', like 'success', 'failure' or 'happiness' means different things to different people, so that defining it is extremely difficult.*

Stress Without Distress. Hans Selye.

Stress is the physical response to a real, or imagined, threat. The human body retains the physical mechanisms needed by primitive people to prepare to meet invaders of their territory by fighting or by running away. The body still follows the 'fight or flight' syndrome when it encounters disturbing circumstances.

The heart rate increases, in order to pump blood more quickly around the body to provide extra energy from the release of stored food. You breathe more quickly to produce more oxygen. Extra adrenalin is produced, muscles tense, the skin sweats to cool you down and the senses become more acute. Although this response is appropriate for *survival,* it is rarely relevant to the actual situation in modern life.

Constant preparation for inappropriate behaviour causes the kind of over-stress which can damage vital systems. As Selye says, stress means different things to different people; some thrive on constant excitement and challenges which would flatten others.

We need a certain amount of stress, to win a tennis match, to encourage us to meet goals or even to motivate us to get up. Too little stress, lack of stimulation or demand, can lead to permanent tiredness and low energy. When the level of stress causes undesirable reactions, which vary for different individuals, there is a risk to general health leading, at its worst, to fatal illness.

Ken Pelletier, in *Mind as Healer, Mind as Slayer* suggests that, during recent years, stress-induced illnesses have replaced infectious diseases as the major medical problems for Western industrial society. The four main areas are cardio-vascular disorders; respiratory diseases like bronchitis; cancer and arthritis.

If everyone in western society is prone to stress, is it undesirable and damaging? Is 'distress' inevitable? How can you tell when stress has reached an undesirable level?

Symptoms of stress

Physical	Thoughts – Emotions
Pounding heart Dry mouth Sweating Lump in throat Butterflies Need to urinate Diarrhoea Queasiness Changed sleeping patterns Changed eating patterns Nightmares Dizziness Loss of sex drive Stuttering Skin problems Muscle aches Backache Headache	Anxiety Apathy Depression Isolation Guilt Nervous tension Anger Fear Difficulty in making decisions Over-sensitivity Inability to concentrate Inability to express thoughts Forgetfulness Paranoia Sadness
Behaviour Restlessness Irritability Accident-prone Nervous laughter Talk too much *or* become silent Overeat, drink or smoke Less committed to work More conflicts Poorer relationships Low output Carelessness Frenetic overwork Obsessions Urge to cry Refusal to go out	**Illness** Asthma Coronary heart disease Ulcers Arthritis linked symptoms Some forms of cancer Migraines Respiratory illnesses

You are unlikely to have all of these at once. Everyone has experienced some of the symptoms, but it is as well to recognise warning signs. If several of these symptoms apply to you, take steps to minimise the effects.

How can I manage stress – are there special techniques?

There are several ways of managing your stress – relaxation, deep breathing, massage, taking a walk, listening to music, talking about your worries. Your lifestyle can help you to prevent unnecessary stress. It is unfortunately and boringly true that only *you* can take responsibility for improving your health and that the steps you need to take appear simple to those who suggest them! Knowing what to do, and doing it, are very different! Everyone knows that smoking is dangerous, but giving up is usually an enormous stuggle. It may be helpful to know that it is never too late to improve your health by giving up smoking, if you could.

Food: Invitations to slim are not simply to make women fit the Miss World stereotype! Overweight people are more likely to be vulnerable to diabetes, arthiritis and coronary heart disease because they are more likely to eat unhealthy food and less likely to take regular exercise.

Drink: Alcohol is acceptable in moderation – unless your religion or your doctor forbid it! The Health Education Authority 'safe' limits allow up to two pints of beer or four measures of spirits, wine or sherry daily for men – half that quantity for women. For reasons not yet fully understood; women have a far lower alcohol tolerance than men.
Most people are surprised to learn that three pints of liquid a day is a desirable minimum to flush the kidneys. Too little water, or liquid, can cause constipation. Drinking a lot of milk, if your diet is otherwise well-balanced, is not particularly healthy because of its fat content. Semi-skimmed is better than full cream milk.

Exercise: There is overwhelming evidence that the body is adversely affected by too little exercise. This does not mean that you must begin to play squash or join an aerobics class! A regular walk, as well as continuing with your present regular activities, like gardening or climbing stairs, will keep your muscles supple.
Physical exertion increases chest expansion, which benefits the lungs and sends more oxygen to the brain. The heart muscles are also stimulated. Obviously, if you are already an active runner, cyclist or games player, you will probably continue, but for the less enthusiastic, jogging is not essential!

A sedentary middle age is an invitation to back pains, heart attacks, broken hips, hernia, arthritis. Yoga and swimming are two of the best physical activities, especially for those over 50. They use every muscle without strain and are at the same time totally relaxing.

Whatever steps you decide to take, do take gentle ones at first.

You are not competing with your youthful self, nor with your children, simply with your desire to sink into an armchair.

Relaxation: Make sure your lifestyle includes activities which relax you. Among the most popular are those related to nature, or to art. Listening to music, gardening, walking in the country, reading, painting or just doing nothing for a few minutes.
Relaxation techniques, deep breathing, yoga and meditation are very helpful, and it is possible to buy cassettes related to these in many health food shops.

Sleep: Make sure you have enough sleep to leave you refreshed on waking. There is no norm; some people are happy with five hours, others need more than seven. The fear of broken nights can sometimes lead to unnecessary dependency on drugs.

Relationships: You need enough people to meet all your needs. Find the courage to tell people you need them, or ask for support if you are feeling low – most people are glad to be able to help.

Believe in the importance of taking care of yourself.

Give yourself treats – your treat may be a cream cake – keep it as an occasional treat – don't turn it into a daily bad habit!

Now you have discovered your own health patterns; you know how well you have been taking care of yourself, and how to prevent unnecessary stress in your life. You are ready to set your goals with your Personal Contract, by writing down any changes you intend to make. Ask someone else to sign the contract and help you to stick to it.

PERSONAL CONTRACT: Taking Care Of Myself

Food:

A I am satisfied with my present lifestyle
B I would like to make some changes:
Tomorrow I will ....

....

Within the next month I will ....

....

Within the next year I will ....

....

Drink:

A I am satisfied with my present lifestyle
B I would like to make some changes:
Tomorrow I will ....

....

Within the next month I will ....

....

Within the next year I will ....

....

Smoking:

A I am satisfied with my present lifestyle
B I would like to make some changes:
Tomorrow I will ....

....

Within the next month I will ....

....

Within the next year I will ....

....

Exercise:

A I am satisfied with my present lifestyle
B I would like to make some changes:
Tomorrow I will ....

....

Within the next month I will ....

....

Within the next year I will ....

....

Recharging:

A I am satisfied with my present lifestyle
B I would like to make some changes:
Tomorrow I will ....

....

Within the next month I will ....

....

Within the next year I will ....

....

People:	A I am satisfied with my present lifestyle B I would like to make some changes: Tomorrow I will .... Within the next month I will .... Within the next year I will ....
Interests:	A I am satisfied with my present lifestyle B I would like to make some changes: Tomorrow I will .... Within the next month I will .... Within the next year I will ....

Signed ____________________________

Witness ____________________ Date ____________________

What Happens If I Feel Ill?

People who are generally healthy, or who do not like to 'make a fuss' need to know which specific signs need medical attention. The following is a **rough** guide:

Anything unusual – sudden change in weight, sleeping, etc.
Bleeding from any orifice.
Prolonged pain.
An increase in conditions you have had for years, e.g. varicose veins which become permanently swollen.
This may seem obvious, but many people assume it is 'normal' for things to get gradually worse.
Learn to distinguish slight from important signs.

Anyone who walks up an unusually steep hill may get a slight pain in the chest. If you get a pain when you climb familiar hills, or the stairs in your house – report it. GPs are more willing nowadays to listen to patients than perhaps they used to be. There is increasing recognition that physical symptoms are possible indicators of emotional distress, but it is important to understand that physical illness still needs treatment ('Psychosomatic' does not mean 'Imaginary'!)

If you feel you are not receiving the kind of attention you would like, you have several options. There are pressure groups to help you – Community Health Councils exist in every Health District, and the Patients' Association, as its name implies, considers complaints made by patients.

If you have been fortunate enough to receive regular health checks through your job, either through private medical insurance, or other arrangements made by employers, you will probably miss this annual reassurance, (some health insurance companies find that as many as 30% of examinations reveal previously unreported symptoms). It would be a positive step in health care if the NHS offered an annual health check. Dentists and opticians are visited regularly for a check-up; babies, and often their mothers, are offered care for the first years, but everyone else seems to visit a GP only when illness is suspected. A thought to pursue with the Patients' Association? An increasing number of GPs now offer older patients a general health check up, either by personal or open invitation. Your Community Health Council should be able to tell you which GPs do.

Why do people use alternative medicine, acupuncture, homeopaths, osteopaths?

Alternative health care increases in popularity and credibility . Most alternative medicine practices are based on the principle of holistic medicine, treating the whole person, not just an individual part, or specific symptoms. This attitude matches the view of health as 'total' mental, physical and emotional well-being, (Pericles' definition of health), and awareness of the links between life experiences, lifestyle and health. Alternative medical practitioners prefer not to use psychotropic drugs, and usually offer an approach which gives time and empathetic attention to the patient. Some of the alternatives, like acupuncture and homeopathy, can be found within the NHS, and some doctors refer patients to osteopaths and even to faith healers. If you decide to seek an alternative to orthodox medicine, try to find a personal recommendation. Properly trained and bona fide practitioners will be listed at their national headquarters.

PROGRESS SUMMARY

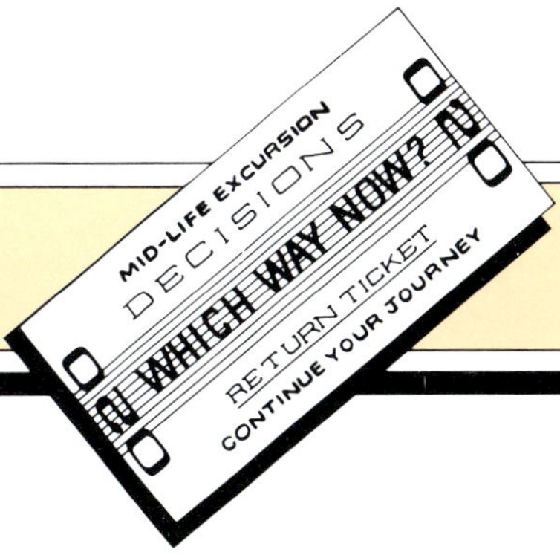

ANALYSIS AND REVIEW OF:

How I take care of myself.
My Health Profile.
Signs and symptoms of stress.
Prevention and management of stress.
My Personal Contract to take care of myself.
Medical advice – alternative medicine.

IMPORTANT INSIGHTS:

I WANT TO CHANGE:

I WANT TO CONTINUE:

I WANT TO BEGIN, OR TO DEVELOP:

NEW FACTS:

LINKS WITH OTHER PAGES:

WHAT'S NEXT? ON TO:
My Philosophy; who do I want to have been? My Obituary.
Coping with disappointment – Putting it all together.

CHAPTER 9

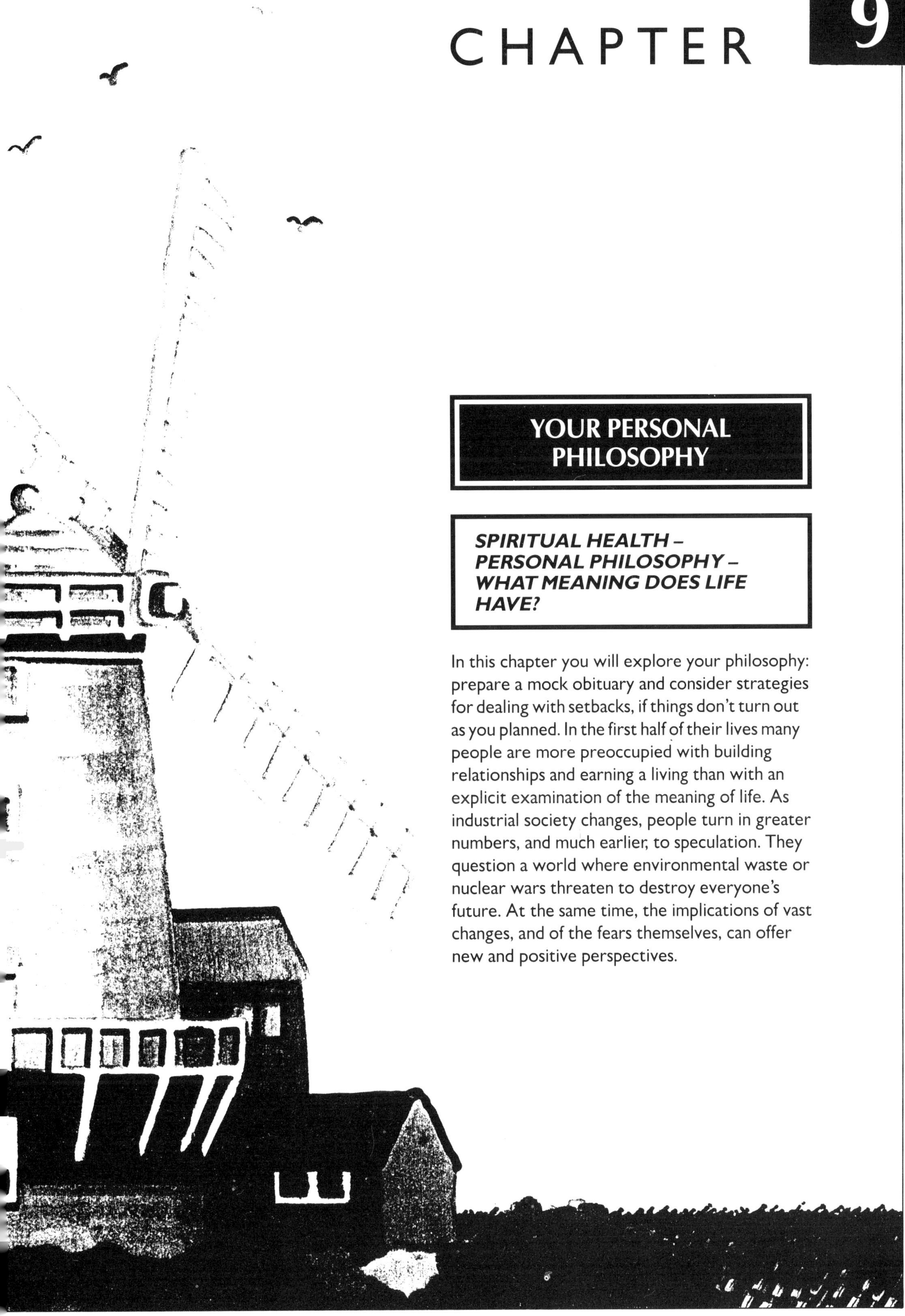

YOUR PERSONAL PHILOSOPHY

SPIRITUAL HEALTH – PERSONAL PHILOSOPHY – WHAT MEANING DOES LIFE HAVE?

In this chapter you will explore your philosophy: prepare a mock obituary and consider strategies for dealing with setbacks, if things don't turn out as you planned. In the first half of their lives many people are more preoccupied with building relationships and earning a living than with an explicit examination of the meaning of life. As industrial society changes, people turn in greater numbers, and much earlier, to speculation. They question a world where environmental waste or nuclear wars threaten to destroy everyone's future. At the same time, the implications of vast changes, and of the fears themselves, can offer new and positive perspectives.

> *Many of the same conditions that produce today's greatest perils also open fascinating new potentials.*

Toffler

Alvin Toffler, in *The Third Wave,* offers a thought–provoking analysis of the future of civilisation.

Religion – life beyond life?

You may draw on a strong religious framework. Those who are active followers of an orthodox religion – Christian, Jewish, Muslim, Hindu, Buddhist, etc., will have based their philosophy and possibly their whole lifestyle on their beliefs.

There are others – humanists, agnostics, atheists, who have a firmly reasoned philosophy based on the finite-ness of life, and have little interest in exploring the possibility of anything beyond death. There does seem to be an inherent desire to re-examine one's beliefs as one reaches the middle years, to read more widely and to reflect as described in the Adult Lifestages 'Restabilisation and Renewal Stage' Chapter 4.

> *And almost everyone, when age,*
> *Disease and sorrows strike him,*
> *Inclines to think there is a God,*
> *Or someone very like Him!*

Dipsychus

People who have reached fifty have lived through or observed the devastation of a number of wars in different parts of the world, have experienced economic depressions and booms, and have seen scientific and technological developments that would have seemed almost inconceivable when they were born. Most of their earlier goals have been achieved or discarded. Few will have escaped the pain of bereavement, which brings sharply into focus the transience of life and a questioning of its purpose. Personal experience of the death of peers makes one aware of the need to use the time that is left well, and of the impossibility of forecasting how much time there might be.

What is the purpose? What are the questions?

You may have more time than before to recall your past dreams and aspirations and perhaps, with the wisdom of maturity, to pursue new patterns of living.

This book has offered you the opportunity to review your own life, What of the lives of others?. . .

Is there a purpose in our existence?

The following questions are not written in the form of an exercise. You will have at some time considered all of them. They are intended to act as a reminder of the underlying dilemmas of being human and your responses will reflect your values and attitudes.

Reflections. . . what is life about?

Is there any purpose in the Universe?
Why do people grow old?
Why do babies become ill and die?
Why do some people recover from serious illness, and others succumb?
Why did the world begin?
When – and how – will it end?
Peace of mind – what is it?
What – and who – do I live for?
Is there anything I would be willing to die for?
What is happiness – love – wisdom?
How should people behave towards each other?
What is equality – can it exist?
What is beauty?
What is truth – is honesty possible?
What is evil – how should it be punished?
What is humour – what purpose does it serve?
What is pleasure?
What if there is, after all, a Plan – or a spiritual future?
Can we ever know? – would we ever want to?
What would make my life even more purposeful than it has been up to now?

(If you would like to continue formal discussion of these issues, you could join an adult education class, the University of the Third Age, Learning in Later Life, etc. See Chapter 7)

The best is yet to come – your goals

> *What you can do, or dream you can, begin it; Boldness has genuis, power and magic in it.*
>
> Goethe

When we are young, there seems to be no limit to our dreams. Many people want to change the world and do manage to change at least a part of it. Most people would like to have made some kind of impact. As middle age arrives, earlier fantasies may seem foolish, or be recalled merely as pleasant dreams. Don't give up too easily! It may still be possible.

A participant in a personal effectiveness workshop confessed that she had always wanted to be a successful artist, but had never had time to paint while her children were at home. She decided to join a local art club and booked a tutored painting holiday in Greece. She now finances her annual painting holidays from the watercolours she sells at the club's exhibitions. She is gaining a considerable reputation as a skilled watercolourist.

My own father-in-law was unable in his youth to become an art teacher. He is now 85 and has been teaching painting to other retired people in Birmingham's Fir Cone. He has had to stop only because his eyesight is failing. The stimulus and satisfaction have led to a retirement which has possibly given him more fulfilment than he found in his job.

The next exercise will help you to clarify some of your early dreams and to see which of your aspirations could still be realised!

EXERCISE 22

LIFETIME AMBITIONS

What to do: Complete the first column, which asks what you wanted to DO, BE, ACHIEVE and POSSESS by the time you were 25. You may not be able to remember exactly, but reflect for a while, it doesn't have to be exactly 25. Then think what your goals might be for the rest of your life – what you want to DO, BE, ACHIEVE and POSSESS. Complete the second column and compare the two columns.

LIFETIME AMBITIONS	
20–25	*By end of life*
DO	**DO**
BE	**BE**
ACHIEVE	**ACHIEVE**
POSSESS	**POSSESS**

EXAMPLE

Jo

20–25		*By end of life*	
DO	*Travel and work abroad for a while. Move in with Peter. Later have two kids. Ban the bomb.*	**DO**	*Leave IBIX on restucturing. Set up my own PR and phone marketing company. See Helen and Timmy happy. Move out of London.*
BE	*A respected journalist. Economically independent. Write for a quality national. The best in my fields.*	**BE**	*Successful head of my own company. Healthy, happy, Grandmother!*
ACHIEVE	*Distinction in my journalism. Editor. A good relationship. Write a novel.*	**ACHIEVE**	*A secure company I can pass on. Time for travel. Write the book. A contented family.*
POSSESS	*Usual things, country cottage, an Aston Martin. Money to do what I want.*	**POSSESS**	*A beautiful garden. a winter home in the Channel Islands. Good friends. Grandchildren.*

What to do next: Answer these questions:

1 How many of your earlier goals have been reached?

....

....

....

2 In what ways is the second column similar to the first?

....

....

....

3 In what ways are they different?

....

....

....

4 Are there any unfulfilled dreams you want to realise?

....

....

....

5 If you have not reached your goals, can you see why?

....

....

....

6 Do your new 'Lifetime Ambitions' reflect your interests, values and skills?

....

....

....

7 How far do your 'Lifetime Ambitions' reflect any decisions you have recently made, or are about to make?

....

....

....

EXAMPLE

Jo

1 *Had two children; haven't written a novel or become top journalist. Didn't marry Peter. Became economically independent. Married Steve and been mostly happy. Had the cottage. Didn't ban the bomb.*
2 *Good relationship. Children. Economic independence. Enough money. At the top in my field.*
3 *Health more important. Career turned out completely differently. Set up house with a different man. Being the boss now much more important. I don't want to work for someone else. Happiness in my family and concern for their well being more important. Creature comforts.*
4 *Yes, plenty. I have yet to set up my company, although plans are well advanced. The move from London. A winter home. Grandchildren. A world safe for them to be born into.*
5 *Yes, I think and plan quite coolly. I made a clear decision not to pursue journalism because of its erratic hours and the need to travel. I also realise that political change is slower and more chaotic than I understood when I was younger.*
6 *Almost exactly – how satisfying!*
7 *Well, obviously, my company plans reflect thinking over the last year or two. And when and where I move will depend on decisions about my company future and the rest of the family. The decisions I am making now will have a big impact on the rest of my life but I am still relatively young.*

Who would you like to have been?. . . become your own clairvoyant. Predict your own future.

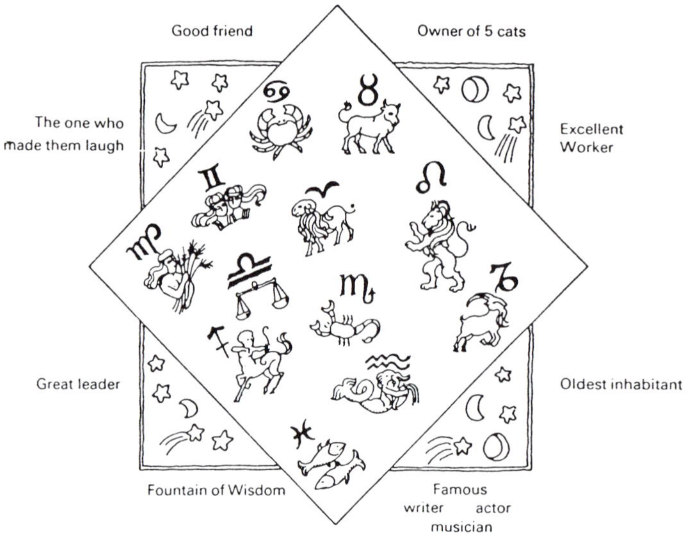

This final section poses the question which enables you to predict the rest of your life. Its objective is to reinforce and summarise all you have discovered and decided, so that you will see how your present decisions match your plan for the future.

> *And were an epitaph to be my story,*
> *I'd have a good one ready for my own,*
> *I'd have it written on me, on my stone,*
> *He had a lover's quarrel with the world.*

Robert Frost

EXERCISE 23

MY OWN OBITUARY*

What to do: Imagine that you are very old and have recently died. Your local newspaper would like to publish an obituary. Write an article of 100–500 words, describing your life.

Include

- where and how you died;
- your health;
- your relationships;
- the kind of person you were;
- what you achieved.

Use your imagination, but keep it within the bounds of possibility. You could run your first marathon at 80 (several people have), but are unlikely to finish first!

EXAMPLE

José Fonesca **Anne Jackson**

José

Choked and died at his 97th birthday party, while responding to a champagne toast. He leaves three daughters, five grandchildren, six great grandchildren and a great-grandson of two weeks. Active to the end, José played the guitar and cycled every day of his life. He spent only two days ever in hospital and never missed a day's work. He retired three times – from the army, from the sports shop he managed, and at the age of 88 from the cycle shop he opened when he was 61. José always had a cheerful word for everyone, and will be sadly missed.

Anne

Grandmother and broadcaster, died last week aged 83. Retiring at 54 from a University post, she travelled the world for two years with her husband. On her return, she wrote two books about her journey and became famous as a lecturer and TV personality. Anne was witty and slightly eccentric, and was last seen on TV a year ago. She and her husband owned a house in London where they entertained family and foreign visitors. She enjoyed food and specialist cooking, but had a weight problem in later life. Her husband died three months ago. Her daughter said today, "She always wanted to go when she did; we'll miss her, she always had a lively interest in everything. We are expecting a large number of people to the funeral, she was active and popular all her life."

*This can be a powerful exercise. Make sure you are feeling positive befor doing it and know that you have someone to talk to if you need to at the end of the exercise.

What to do next: Read through your obituary and answer the questions:

1 How much of your obituary is fact?

....

....

....

2 Do you want your predictions to come true?

....

....

....

3 What has prevented you in the past from reaching your goals?
A External – e.g. Money, health, opportunity.
B Internal – e.g. Fear, other people's opinions, lack of confidence.

....

....

....

4 What might prevent you in the future?

....

....

....

5 How do you plan to carry out your intentions?

....

....

....

6 Comparing your 'Obituary' with your 'Lifetime Ambitions', what similarities do you see?

....

....

....

EXAMPLE

José Anne

José

Not yet done

1 *Learned to play the guitar. Had great-grandchildren. Bought a cycle shop.*

Do I want all this?

2 *Wouldn't mind if it did all happen.*

What has prevented it?

3 *Too busy working – never found time for a guitar, but plan to learn now. Only one of my sons has children yet, but I'm hoping!*

I was offered the job in the sports shop. I only recently thought about a cycle shop when I finally leave here.

What might prevent it?

4 *Guitar – nothing. New babies – have to rely on my children! But I love the company of the young, and I suppose it's one way of ensuring my name carries on. I could teach them all to ride bikes! Don't know if I can afford a cycle shop. Health or accident in some way, but I'm a very fit man and a great optimist.*

How will you make it happen?

5 *L.E.A. – Guitar classes. Persuade my family that kids are 'a good thing' and be a helpful, but not interfering, grandparent.*

Keeping the 'bike shop' quiet, but I suppose I could enquire through customers, friends, Small Firms Service or follow a 'Start-Up' course. Whether it's a shop or not, I like to think I'll work forever!

Comparison

6 *Very similar, to stay as healthy as I am now; to cycle up to the day I die; to go on enjoying life and to die while I'm happy!*

Anne

Not yet done

1 *Travelled the world, written the books, become a TV personality. Been widowed.*

Do I want all this?

2 *All except the weight problem.*

What has prevented it?

3 *Have travelled, and written a few stories – no one asked me to be on TV; somehow too busy to write the book. I have planned to use some of my new leisure time to write.*

What might prevent it?

4 *I see no reason why any of those things are impossible. I suppose it's a bit cheeky to expect to become a TV personality, but recognition is one of my values. I can't visualise being without my husband, and hope there will always be people around. I want to go on entertaining but I'm afraid I will put on weight.*

How will you make it happen?

5 *We have arranged to spend at least six months abroad. I intend to write a book eventually. Looking at my answer to 4, I suppose I must take care of my weight!*

Comparison

6 *To go round the world. I've wanted that since I was 14. I have envied my children and their friends their travel opportunities.*

Putting it all together – images and attitudes

You have now reached the end of your self review. Look back over these exercises and draw up a summary of how you see yourself and your attitudes in different aspects of your life.

Summary after final reflections

I am satisfied with my attitudes towards:

....

....

....

....

I would like to change my attitudes towards:

....

....

....

....

I will need to watch out for these danger signals:

....

....

....

....

I've made all these plans – what if something goes wrong?

What might stop you getting you what you want?

- Lack of confidence.
- Lack of skill.
- Change in personal circumstances – relationships.
  - financial.
  - environment.
- Health.
- National and world events.
- Acts of God; – 'Fire, flood and tempest-type' events.

When anything happens to prevent a planned activity, it is important to see, first, which of these factors is operating – it may be more than one.

You need to know how you respond to setbacks.

EXERCISE 24

SETBACKS – MY RESPONSES

What to do: Complete the following sentences.

When I don't get something I have planned and worked for, I. . . .

Say ....

....

Think ....

....

Feel ....

....

Do ....

....

Believe ....

....

If I make mistakes, I. . . .

Say (to myself) ....

....

Think ....

....

Feel ....

....

Do ....

....

Believe ....

....

What to do next: Read the next section, on self-defeating behaviour, then compare your own reactions to see where you could make more positive responses to disappointments and setbacks.

EXAMPLE

James

Event:	**Setback:**	
Holiday booked	Broken Leg	**Say:** Oh no! Damn. **Think:** Just my luck – probably my fault. **Feel:** Guilty, self-pity. **Do:** Cancel the booking, contact insurance. **Believe:** It is outside my control.

Managing setbacks and disappointments

If you do not achieve what you planned, you can always repeat some of the exercises, to see if there are options. You can also discover your own pattern of response to setbacks.

Belief barrier. . . it interferes with all the others!

This includes thinking, feeling and telling ourselves we are wrong. We all tend to give ourselves negative messages when things go wrong – I've failed again, I'm stupid, I never do anything properly, I'm careless, thoughtless. . . . and on, and on, and on. . . .

How to break down the barrier

Change the message you give yourself: and listen to what you say!

- I did my best, but it didn't happen.
- I made a mistake.
- I'm disappointed and angry, and that's normal and acceptable.
- I don't want to be perfect – I'm a human.
- I will see if I can avoid this mistake next time.
- Sometimes I just have to be disappointed – in time I will accept this.

Constant negative thinking lowers self-esteem and you may refuse to take further risks, even tiny ones.

Know what your feelings are

Acknowledge and accept your disappointment, anger, hurt.
Talk to someone about them – a member of your personal network.
If necessary, talk to someone who is professionally able to help.

Managing setbacks – detailed strategies

You need to manage three aspects –

The Emotional	**The Rational**	**The Practical**
How you feel	What you think	What needs to be done

When you have dealt with your emotional reaction, you will be ready to think about your next practical move. There are six stages:

1 Re-appraise your decision.

2 Re-appraise your interests – skills – objectives.

3 Think if *you* did anything to influence the setback.

4 Think how much was due to unavoidable external circumstances.

5 Think of other ways to reach your objective (contingency plan).

6 If this fails, set a new objective.

EXAMPLE

Theo

Theo's decision to play regular golf and learn German to strengthen his application for promotion to European marketing manager in 1992 received a setback. Theo broke both his legs in a car crash and was housebound for weeks. He could not go to his German classes, and would probably not be able to play golf for a very long time, if ever.

1 Re-appraise the decision
I may never be strong enough to walk round a course again, but I don't want to leave the club, neither do I want to fall behind with my German studies.

2 Re-appraise objectives
Maintain my fitness, companions, interests, skills, stimulus. I still want to do this.

3 My part in the setback
Only insofar as I went out on very icy roads when I was advised it was dangerous.

4 External
The weather, the surface of the roads, being on my own, so no-one found me for half-an-hour.

5 Other Ways – contingency plan

1 *Get someone to push my wheelchair to the golf club. When I am better, take a voluntary job there. Practise walking, contact the Sports Council, find other ways to keep fit.*
2 *Ask if the German class can meet in my home.*
3 *Get German records and textbooks and ask one or two class members to practise with me.*
4 *Find out everything I can about recovery from broken bones.*
5 *Ask the local Council to provide better services in bad weather. Write to my local paper.*

Managing setbacks – summary sheet

1 I have discovered that I usually deal with setbacks by:

....

(See also Chapter 3 Managing Transitions.)

2 Messages I usually hear:

....

3 Messages I plan to hear

A...

B ....

C...

4 The most important members of my personal network are:

....

....

5 I already have contingency plans for .... of my current goals. If anything unexpected happens, I will first:

....

....

PROGRESS SUMMARY

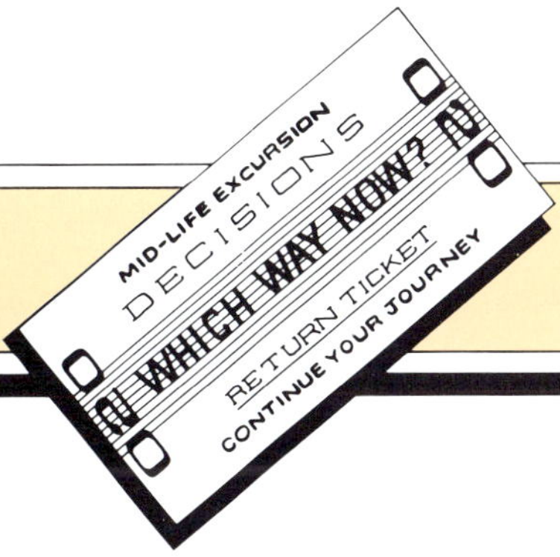

ANALYSIS AND REVIEW OF:

Philosophy.
Lifetime Ambitions – Final Reflections.
Strategies for Managing Setbacks.

IMPORTANT INSIGHTS:

I WANT TO CHANGE:

I WANT TO CONTINUE:

I WANT TO BEGIN, OR TO DEVELOP:

NEW FACTS:

LINKS WITH OTHER PAGES:

WHAT'S NEXT? ON TO: Resources – books and addresses.

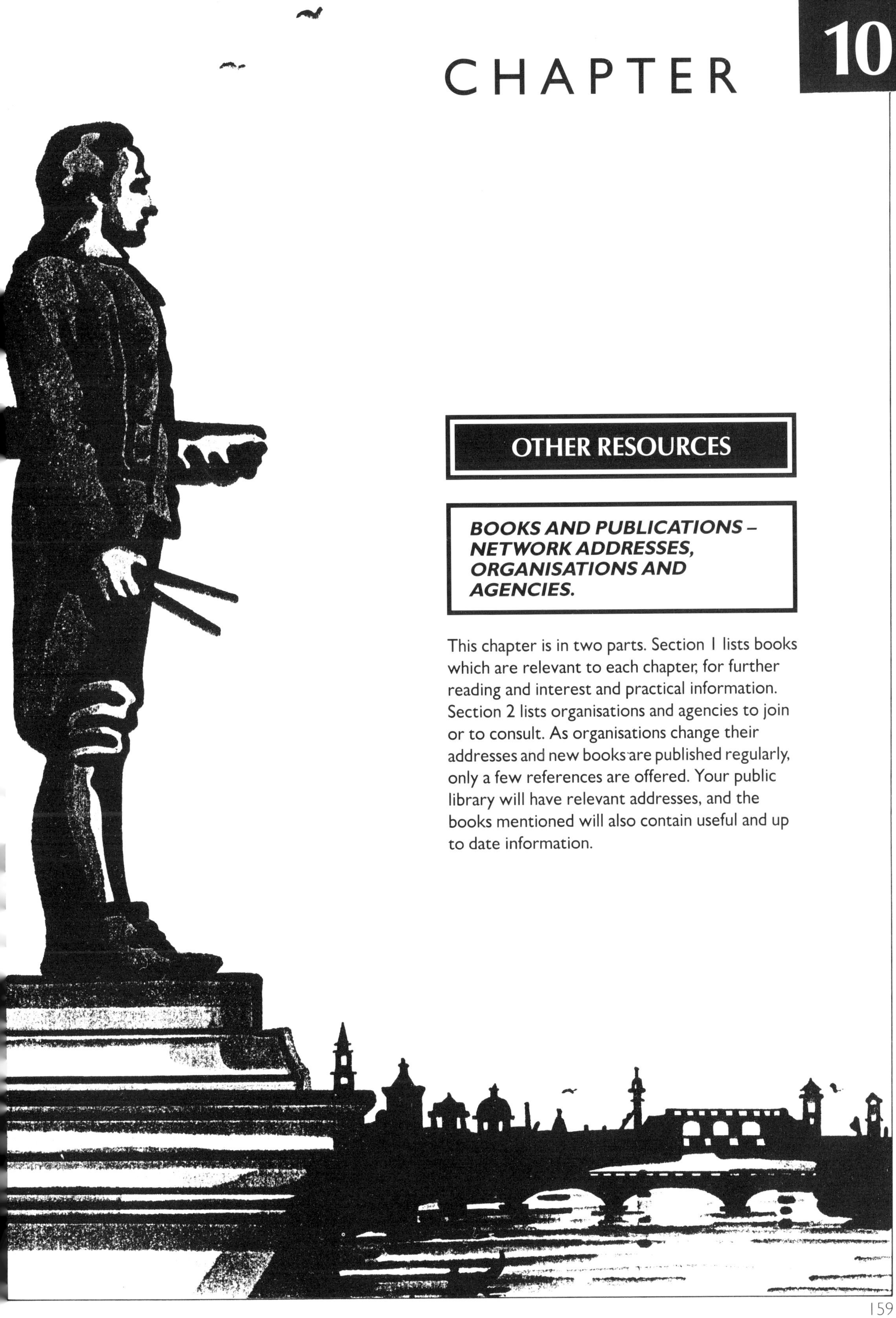

CHAPTER 10

OTHER RESOURCES

BOOKS AND PUBLICATIONS – NETWORK ADDRESSES, ORGANISATIONS AND AGENCIES.

This chapter is in two parts. Section 1 lists books which are relevant to each chapter, for further reading and interest and practical information. Section 2 lists organisations and agencies to join or to consult. As organisations change their addresses and new books are published regularly, only a few references are offered. Your public library will have relevant addresses, and the books mentioned will also contain useful and up to date information.

Section 1

Books and Publications

CHAPTER 1 INTRODUCTION

Handy, Professor C	Taking Stock – Being Fifty in the Eighties	BBC Publications, 1983
Higgins, R	The Seventh Enemy	Hodder & Stoughton, 1978
Jenkins, C & Sherman, B	The Collapse of Work	Eyre Methuen, 1979
Toffler, A	Future Shock The Third Wave	Pan Books, 1970 Pan Books, 1980

CHAPTER 2 HOW DO I FEEL ABOUT MY FUTURE? CAN I AFFORD TO CHANGE?

Gilkes, A G & Sinclair, R	Hambro's Tax Guide	Robert Yeatman
Rudinger, E (Ed.)	Wills and Probate	Consumers Assoc. 1983
Spiers, B & P & Jewell, P	Early Retirement on Medical Grounds	G.L.A.P. 19 St Margaret, Pattens Church, Eastcheap, EC3M 1HS
	Money Which	Consumers Assoc.
Clutterbuck, D & HIll, R	The Remaking of Work	Grant McIntyre 1981
Maslow, A	Farther Reaches of Human Nature	Penguin 1971

CHAPTER 3 THE MANAGEMENT OF CHANGE

Hill, Susan	In the Springtime of the Year	Penguin, 1977

CHAPTER 4 THE MIDDLE YEARS – MAKING THE MOST OF THEM

Cooper, Wendy	No change	Arrow books
Franks, Helen	Prime Time: The Mid-Life Woman in Focus	Pan
Levinson, D J	Seasons of a Man's Life	Knopf (New York) 1978
MacDonald, Janet	Climbing the Ladder. How to be a Woman Manager	Methuen
Martin, Jean & Roberts, Ceidwen	Women and Employment: A Lifetime Perspective	Dept of Employment OPCS 1980
Phillips, A & Rakusen, J	Our Bodies, Our Selves	Penguin 1979
Robertson, J	A Sane Alternative	Turning Point, 9 New Road, Ironbridge, Shropshire
Sheehy, Gail	Passages Pathfinders	Bantam 1982 Bantam 1983

CHAPTER 5 WHO ELSE IS THERE IN MY LIFE?

Comfort, Alex	The Joy of Sex	Quartet Books
Dickson, Anne	A Woman in Your Own Right	Quartet Books
Shapiro, Jean, Ed.	On Your Own (for women)	Pandora 1984

CHAPTER 6 WHAT AM I LIKE? WHAT DOES THIS MEAN TO ME?

Bolles, R N	Three Boxes of Life	Ten Speed Press 1982
Bolles, R N	What Colour is Your Parachute?	Ten Speed Press 1988
Francis, Dave	Manage Your Own Career	Fontana 1985
Hopson, B & Scally, M	Lifeskills Teaching Programmes Nos. 1-4	Lifeskills Associates 1988
Hopson, B & Scally, M	Build Your Own Rainbow	Lifeskills Associates 1984
Laikein, A	How To Get Control of Your Time and Your Life	Signet 1983

CHAPTER 7 WHAT ARE MY PRACTICAL OPTIONS?

General

Nathan, R & Syrett, M	How to Survive Unemployment	Penguin 1983
Germann, R & Arnold, P	Job and Career Building	Ten Speed Press 1982

Paid Work

Brady, C	A Bit On The Side	Collins 1983
Gray, M	Working from Home – 201 Ways to Earn Money	Judy Piatkus, Leighton, Essex
Department of Environment	Letting Rooms In Your Home	Fontana, 1982
Rudinger, E (Ed)	Earning Money at Home	Consumers Assoc
Sunday Times	The Good Job Guide	New Opportunity Press
P.E.R.	A Guide to Successful Job-Hunting	Free from P.E.R.
P.E.R.	Jobkey	Free from P.E.R.

Self-Employment

Barrow, C	BBC Small Business Guide	BBC Publications 1982
Golzen, G	Working for Yourself	Daily Telegraph 1983
	Working Abroad – Daily Telegraph Guide to Working & Living Overseas	Daily Telegraph

Rudinger, E (Ed)	Starting Your Own Business	Consumers Assoc
Woodcock, C	Guardian Guide to Running a Small Business	Kogan Page
	Co-operatives	
Cockerton et. al.	Workers Co-operatives, a Handbook	Peoples' Press 1980
	Unpaid Work	
Gundrey, E	Sparing Time – Observer Guide to Helping Others	Unwin Paperback
Kirby, J	Work After Work	Quiller Press 1984
	Someone Like You Can Help – A Guide to Voluntary Organisations	London Council of Social Service
	Voluntary Social Services. A Directory of National Organisations	N.C.S.S. 26 Bedford Square, LONDON W1
	Leisure	
Rapoport, R & R N	Leisure and the Family Life-cycle	Routledge & Kegan Paul
	Learning	
Buzan, T	Use Your Head	BBC Publications 1980
	Directory of Further Education	CRAC, Cambridge

CHAPTER 8 DO I TAKE CARE OF MYSELF?

Benson, H	The Relaxation Response	Avon Books 1976
Gore, I	Age and Vitality	Unwin Paperbacks 1979
Hanson, Dr Peter	The Joy of Stress	Pan 1986
Iyengar, B K S	Light On Yoga	Unwin Paperbacks 1980
Livingstone Booth, A	Stressmanship	Severn House Publishers Ltd 1985
Pelletier, K	Mind As Healer, Mind As Slayer	Alan & Unwin 1979
Rudinger, E (Ed)	Living with Stress	Consumers Assoc
Stoppard, Dr Miriam	Fifty Plus Life Guide	Dorling Kindersley 1983
Wright, B	Health Choices: O.U. Short Course Community Education	Open University PO Box 76, Walton Hall, Milton Keynes MK7 6AA

Fromm, E	The Art of Loving To Have or to Be	Unwin Paperbacks Unwin Paperbacks
Jung, C	Man and his Symbols	Aldus Books 1964
Kelly, G	A Theory of Personality	National Library 1963
Rogers, C	On Personal Power	Constable & Co 1978
Ronson, R	Second Time Around (A Practical Guide To Beginning Life Again)	David & Charles 1986

Section 2

Network Addresses: Organisations and Agencies

Your local DSS office	See telephone directory
Disability Alliance (produce an excellent handbook)	See telephone directory
Inland Revenue	See telephone directory

(SEE ALSO: Citizen's Advice Bureau; Welfare Rights Offices; Law Centres. Addresses from the telephone directory, public library or town hall.)
Many of these organisations have local branches, so do ask at your public library, local town hall or Citizen's Advice Bureau. If they cannot help you, then write to the address given here, remembering to enclose a stamped addressed envelope.

Personal relationships

Relate (formerly National Marriage Guidance Council)	7A Sheep Street, Rugby

Caring for elderly relatives

Age Concern England	Bernard Sunley House, Pitcairn Road, Mitcham, Surrey
National Association of Carers	58 New Road, Chatham, Kent, ME4 4QR
National Council for the Single Woman and her Dependants	29 Chilworth Mews, London W2 3RG
National Council for Carers and their Elderly Dependants	29 Chilworth Mews, London W2 3RG

Bereavement and loneliness

CRUSE (Support and advice for the bereaved)	CRUSE House, Sheen Road, Richmond, Surrey
Old Friends – Introduction Agency for the over 40s	18a Highbury New Park, London N5 2DB
Samaritans	See telephone directory, or: 17 Uxbridge Road, Slough SL1 1AN

Moving house

National Federation of Housing Associations	30–32 Southampton Street, London WC2F 7HF

Paid employment – full and part–time

Buretire Ltd	The Employment Fellowship, Drayton House, Gordon Street, WC1
Executive Standby	310 Chester Road, Hartford, Northwich, CW8 2AB Somercourt, Homefield Road, Salford, Bristol, BS18 3EG 51 London Wool Exchange, Brushfield Street, E1
Federation of Personnel Services (Lists approved Employment/Counselling Agencies – although non-members may be highly reputable!)	120 Baker Street, London W1M 2DE
Job Centres	Telephone directory or public library
Job-sharing Project – New Ways to Work	347A Upper Street, London N1 OPD
Opportunities for the Disabled	1 Bank Building, Princes Street, London EC2 8EU
Part-Time Careers Ltd	10 Golden Square, London W1R 2AF
Professional and Executive Recruitment (P.E.R.)	Ask at Job Centre for address of the nearest centre – there are over 30 nationwide
Royal Association of Disability and Rehabilitation (RADAR)	25 Mortimer Street, London W1
Success After Sixty (for over 50s!)	40–41 Old Bond Street, London W1X 3AP

Self-Employment – Small Businesses

Business in the Community (will give addresses of local Enterprise Agencies)	91 Waterloo Road, London, SE1 8XP
Rural Development Commission (RDC)	141 Castle Street, Salisbury, Wilts. SP1 3TP
Confederation of British Industry, Small Firms Council	Centrepoint, New Oxford Street, London WC1
Crafts Council	12 Waterloo Place, London SW1Y 4AV
London Enterprise Agency	69 Cannon Street, London EC4 5AB
National Chamber of Trade	Enterprise House, Henley–on–Thames, Oxon, RG6 1TV

National Federation of Self-Employed and Small Businesses Ltd	32 St Annes Road West, Lytham St Annes, Lancs. FY8 1NY
New Enterprise Network	3 Stonehill, Chobham, Surrey, GU24 8HP
Development Board for Rural Wales	Ladywell House, Newton, Powys, SY16 1JB
Small Business Unit, Welsh Development Agency	Treforest Industrial Estate, Pontypridd, Mid-Glamorgan CF37 UJ
Northern Ireland Development Board	Local Enterprise Development Unit, Lamont House, Purdys Lane, Belfast BT8 17 The Diamond, Londonderry, BP48 6BR
Scottish Development Agency	102 Telford Road, Edinburgh EH4 2NP
Small Business Division	20 Bothwell Street, Glasgow
Highlands and Islands Development Board	Bridge House, Bank Street, Inverness, IV1 1QR
Scottish Retail Federation	203 Pitt Street, Glasgow GL2 7JG
Small Business Bureau	32 Smith Square, London WC1P 3HH
Small Firms Centres	FREEFONE 2444 (wherever you live)
Small Firms Division, Department of Industry	Abell House, John Islip, London, SW1P 4LN
URBED	359 Strand, London, WC2 OHP
Women in Enterprise	26 Bond Street, Wakefield, W. Yorks (and local offices)
Women into Business	32 Smith Square, London, WC1P 3HH

Co-operatives

Beechwood College	Elmete Lane, Leeds LS8 2LQ
Co-operative Development Agency	20 Albert Embankment, London, SE1 71J
Industrial Common Ownership Movement (ICOM)	7–8 The Corn Exchange, Leeds, LS1 7BP

Unpaid Work

Very few individual voluntary organisations are listed. Public libraries have lists of all organisations which welcome offers of help, and there may be a Volunteer Bureau in your area. The addresses given below, together with the books in Section 1 cover work at home or overseas, and should provide most of the information you might need.

British Executive Service Overseas	116 Pall Mall, London, SW1Y 5ED
Central Register of Charities	Charity Commissioners, 57 Haymarket, London SW1 OPZ
Community Service Volunteers (Some schemes for over 50s)	237 Pentonville Road, London NW1
International Voluntary Service	0554 IVS, 53 Report Road, Leicester

London Voluntary Service Council	68 Chalton Street, London NW1 1JR
National Council of Voluntary Organisations	26 Bedford Square, London WC1B 3HV
OXFAM Voluntary Service Council	68 Chalton Street, London NW1 1JR
Retired Executives Action Clearing House (REACH)	Victoria House, Southampton Row, London WC1
Voluntary Service Overseas	19 Lower Belgrave Street, London SW1W OLR